REFLECTIONS
EIGHT KING HENRYS

*Leaves of Time – main leaf in watercolour,
others are pressed motifs by artist Elaina.*

REFLECTIONS
EIGHT KING HENRYS

TIMOTHY GILBERT

BREWIN BOOKS

BREWIN BOOKS
19 Enfield Ind. Estate,
Redditch,
Worcestershire,
B97 6BY
www.brewinbooks.com

Published by Brewin Books 2024

© Timothy Gilbert, 2024

The author has asserted his rights in accordance with the
Copyright, Designs and Patents Act 1988 to be
identified as the author of this work.

All rights reserved. No part of this publication may be
reproduced, stored in a retrieval system, or transmitted in any
form or by any means, electronic, mechanical, photocopying,
recording or otherwise, without the prior permission in writing
of the publisher and the copyright owners, or as expressly
permitted by law, or under terms agreed with the appropriate
reprographics rights organisation. Enquiries concerning
reproduction outside the terms stated here should be sent to the
publishers at the UK address printed on this page.

The publisher makes no representation, express or implied,
with regard to the accuracy of the information contained in
this book and cannot accept any legal responsibility for any
errors or omissions that may be made.

A CIP catalogue record for this book is available
from the British Library.

ISBN: 978-1-85858-774-5

Printed and bound in Great Britain
by Halstan & Co. Ltd.

CONTENTS

AUTHOR'S NOTE

The rich diversity of monarchs bearing the name 'Henry' (the meaning is 'ruler of the home') first drew me to this project. If 'home' by extension is taken as 'realm', it will be seen that these men were not – to put it mildly! – allotted an equal measure of governing capability. My hope is that the 'general reader', whoever she or he may be, will be stimulated by the pages that follow to pursue enquiries of their own.

I am not an academic specialist; I write rather as a student with an interest in the period of the English kings called Henry, 1100-1547 (with breaks), who has read widely over several decades. Between 1272 and 1399 there were no Henrys; however, the fateful and tumultuous nature of those times – in particular the Great Famine and the Black Death – seemed to call for what I have termed a connecting 'bridge passage'. I hope that there may even be a semblance of a narrative thread running through the pages.

There have been no family members (de rigueur, it would seem, with most writers) to 'chivvy me along', still less to offer fortifying mugs of green tea at 2.30 a.m. as I grappled with the issues. Instead I took heart from some words of Dr Samuel Johnson: 'a man may always write when he will set himself doggedly to it.'

I am deeply grateful to James Simister, Julia Holding, Joe Ellison and Vernon Small for reading the text and for their valuable comments. Luigi rendered invaluable service in the production of the text. Thanks also are due to Elaina for the art work. For any 'howlers' (as a brutish French schoolmaster would call them), solecisms and stupidities that remain, I take full responsibility.

Many of the ideas and turns of phrase, jotted down on scraps of paper and written up afterwards, came to me on board the 529 bus service to Wolverhampton. So here let me pay my own tribute to the dedicated drivers on that justly celebrated route.

I dedicate this book to the memory of my friends Lauren Dennis and Nigel Fortune.

Epiphany 2024

1066 AND THE AFTERMATH

The Normans successfully invaded England in 1066. Harold, the last Saxon king, was killed at Hastings, along with many of his comrades-in-arms.

Duke William of Normandy had contended that the English throne was his as of right, according to the wishes of the late king, Edward the Confessor; Harold had committed perjury – he had sworn an oath to support William's succession. William's claim was upheld by the pope and therefore, it might be presumed, by God also. Victory at Hastings was seen as further vindication of the justice of his cause. Still, the truth of the matter was hotly disputed. Duke William's claim did not go uncontested.

Saxon England was perhaps the most efficiently organised polity in Western Europe at the time: shires, administered by shire-reeves, systems of regional courts and royal taxation were all in place. There was a commitment to the rule of law and the principle of judicial fairness. Education and learning were encouraged. The reigns of such outstanding kings as Alfred the Great (died 899) and also his son Edward the Elder (died 924), best known for repulsing the Vikings, were crucial in the formation of a single, south-centred Anglo-Saxon kingdom.

It is hardly surprising then that the imposition of the 'Norman yoke' was bitterly resented. William's comrades and associates set about ruthlessly appropriating lands from their previous owners.

Others, such as clerics, administrators and the like, soon crossed the Channel in their wake.

The 'Harrying of the North' during the winter of 1069-1070 is a particular blot on William's record. Local rebellions, encouraged by the Scots and the Danes, led to a brutal military campaign of slaughter and pillage to subjugate northern England; it may justly be called a policy of 'scorched earth'.

In retrospect we know that William prevailed, but in 1066 there was no necessary reason to believe it would be so. As late as 1086 – William died the following year – Canute IV of Denmark was murdered while planning an invasion of England.

The Domesday Book (its findings seen as no less definitive than the Last Judgement), completed in 1086 on William's orders, cannot be viewed in isolation from his security concerns. This Great Survey, the defining document of the reign, set out to assess the wealth and assets of the king's subjects throughout the land. It was designed for fiscal purposes, to protect and increase his revenue; William needed to raise taxes to pay for his army. A huge amount of land in England had changed hands since the Conquest. A record of these changes was essential. This survey, quite unprecedented in scale and ambition, helped William to maintain control throughout his kingdom.

England was, in relative terms, a wealthy country and taking it over proved to be a good investment. Estimates of population are notoriously uncertain. A figure of a little under 2 million in 1066 may be cautiously suggested. This would rise significantly in the following 200 years (at the very least it doubled) and was the key to driving forward the economy, the stimulus to production.

The year 1066 marked the start of a long period in which the king of England was also ruler of a substantial territory in France. Many important members of the Anglo-Norman baronage held land on both sides of the Channel. This Anglo-Norman order, a political entity ruled by Frenchmen, endured until the 1140s. This was the world that our first king called Henry, as he came to maturity, would have known.

CHAPTER 1

HENRY I (1100-1135)

Henry I

Henry was the youngest of the three surviving sons of William I, the Conqueror (1066-1087). He was a rather unexpected king of England but would become one of its most outstanding. Contemporaries certainly took a broadly favourable view of this 'lion of justice' – 'No one dared injure another in his time', wrote the Anglo-Saxon chronicler.

On 2 August 1100 the king, William II ('Rufus'), was in the New Forest. It was the start of the hunting season; many of William's friends and the great men of the realm, including Henry himself, were present. Tragically, the king was killed by a stray arrow. Accidents were not uncommon, and this was almost certainly one of them.

It might be thought that Henry's other brother Robert Curthose (his father's nickname meaning 'short stockings') would now inherit the Conqueror's domains, but he was returning from the Crusade – and his present whereabouts were unknown. Henry was the man on the spot and he acted decisively; he went with haste to Winchester to secure the royal treasury, and on 5 August he was crowned king. It was not absolutely accepted that sons would succeed in order of seniority, so Henry was not behaving wholly improperly. Additionally, he had been born 'in the purple': that is, after his father had become king of England. Inevitably, in the circumstances of life, Henry's relationship with his elder brothers had not always been easy and he had himself suffered imprisonment at Curthose's hands. The Conqueror had left him a cash fortune but no land; Robert had been granted Normandy, which he subsequently mortgaged to Rufus in return for 10,000 marks to finance his part in the Crusade. Still, this was not a situation that Robert, on his return, was likely to find tolerable.

One of the better things about the Normans was their general reluctance, unless absolutely necessary, to engage in pitched battle. (Another good point is that a certain code of chivalry was observed; from 1077 to 1306 no earl was executed in England.) Battles were desperately uncertain affairs, involving potential loss of life, lands, castles and freedom. Quite often some 'deal' was brokered. And so it now proved.

Henry's elaborate Coronation Charter, repudiating Rufus' notorious abuses, was issued on the day of his crowning. This was something of a departure – a manifesto addressed to the shires, to the whole political community. There would be none of his brother's oppressions. The new king would not exploit ecclesiastical vacancies; all unjust financial exactions would be abolished; Henry would also be a good lord to his men by limiting the powers he claimed over marriage and inheritance and the contributions he would levy from them. 'I establish a firm peace in all my kingdom, and I order that this peace shall henceforth be kept.' This, as events turned out, was to be the greatest achievement of his reign. This document was sent to each of the shires.

Henry's situation at the start of his reign, though, was desperately insecure. The return of Anselm, the saintly and revered archbishop of Canterbury and a committed supporter of the new king, was deeply significant in strengthening waverers among Henry's baronage. Robert, count of Meulan, a man renowned for his intelligence and sagacity across the Anglo-Norman world, was another key adherent, and he remained Henry's chief counsellor until his life's end. Still, Robert Curthose, as the elder brother and a renowned crusader, also had very significant levels of support among the nobility.

Robert duly landed at Portsmouth with an army in July 1101. After some hard bargaining, an agreement was reached at Alton: Robert renounced his claim to England during Henry's lifetime and also that of any heir born to him; in return Henry – clearly the winner – granted his brother cash and a pension. Robert's drawing back from a military showdown with his brother probably disgusted his baronial supporters; he returned to Normandy, a diminished figure.

Henry's brother Rufus, a hot-blooded though effective ruler with an apparently mocking sense of humour, had not been popular with the monastic chroniclers of the time. He was widely believed to utter profanities. To put it mildly, Rufus was far more at home in the rude company of his camp followers than with august clerics. His wretched end might be perceived as God's judgement upon an unworthy life. Vacant church livings, bishoprics and abbeys especially, were left unfilled, their revenues accruing to the crown. Anselm, with whom Rufus had had a torrid relationship, had gone into self-imposed exile. Now Henry desperately wanted to draw a line under this friction with the Church and to place things on a business footing. 'Business' actually sums up Henry rather neatly; there was always an air of calculation about the man.

Then an unexpected problem arose for Henry, and possibly Anselm too: the Investiture Controversy. This related to the claim made by lay rulers to invest an abbot – or bishop-elect – with the ring and pastoral staff and to receive homage from him before his consecration: a practice condemned by the pope three decades earlier. Eventually, in 1105, a compromise in England was reached on obvious lines: Henry renounced the investiture whilst retaining the homage. The whole business certainly muddied the waters when a fresh start to the church-state relationship was both needed and desired.

It seems possible that Anselm had a genuine regard, as well as a wary admiration, for Henry. The archbishop saw him as the man who would end what he regarded as Rufus' oppressive treatment of the Church; and, unlike Duke Robert in Normandy, he proved himself to be an effective ruler, bringing order and stability.

In 1100 Anselm sanctioned the marriage of Henry and Edith, soon to be known as Matilda, a member of the Scottish royal house who was also descended from the pre-Conquest English ruling house. The union certainly made political sense (always a characteristic of Henry) in uncertain times and enhanced his position, but it was still controversial as Edith had been a nun, a 'bride of Christ'. The case of its proponents therefore, pre-eminently Anselm himself, had to be that she had never been a nun at all and that she had only spent some years disguised as one for her own safety. Possibly, too, the pastor in Anselm hoped that such a marriage might enable the king to practise continence (Henry acknowledged over 20 illegitimate children); if so, the archbishop, fundamentally a realist and certainly nobody's fool, cannot have been over-optimistic! With his queen, Henry had a daughter and a son: Matilda, who was married to the German emperor Henry V when she was not yet 12; and William, his heir and the hope of the dynasty.

The battle of Tinchebrai (1106) in Normandy was crucial for the future of the Anglo-Norman world. Duke Robert, though a renowned crusader knight, had shown himself incapable of governing the strife-ridden duchy effectively. Henry intervened to decisive effect: he took control of Normandy and thus reunited his father's lands. This did much to reduce the sense of political insecurity felt by the great men who held lands on both sides of the Channel. Robert was imprisoned for life, though his confinement was probably 'honourable'. It was reported that he lived in considerable luxury in the bishop of Salisbury's magnificent castle at Devizes, where he was detained for some years. That Robert lived well into his eighties – remarkable enough for the times – dying only the year before Henry, certainly suggests that even in captivity he was well enough treated.

'Stern', 'harsh', 'relentless': such is how Henry has sometimes been characterised by much later writers. It is a well-known fact that false moneyers were mutilated, though such sanctions were in accord with traditional English laws against false coins; the Anglo-Saxon chronicler spoke approvingly of this sternness. The 'defenestration' (throwing from a window) for treason of Conan, a citizen of Rouen, is cited as evidence of Henry's cruelty; but

Conan was a bourgeois, a commoner, for whom different rules clearly applied, and this was treason.

Roger, bishop of Salisbury and a man of outstanding ability, was pre-eminent among Henry's servants, and provided essential continuity and expertise throughout the reign. Roger headed both the judicial and financial administration, and he also presided over the exchequer, first mentioned in 1110, and so called from the chequered counting cloth on which all transactions were recorded. The results of this annual royal audit were recorded on a great roll (the 'Pipe Roll'); a new one was opened for every year: the one for 1130 is the first to survive, and the only one from Henry's reign. The Pipe Rolls were originally rolls of sheepskin, recording moneys received twice a year by the treasury from the sheriffs of the shires. Land was by far the largest component of the king's total income. The office of treasurer of the chamber appears for the first time in the 1120s. The work of the chancellor expanded.

Justices were sent on circuits round the shires to hear crown pleas and civil business that were brought before them; these royal servants became largely responsible for the administration of royal justice in the shires. The business of the courts was to be 'my pleas' and 'my judgements' (Henry was always fond of the first person!). Everyone was subject to the king's justice. Anyone of the court found guilty of plundering the countryside and peasantry as it moved around – a charge particularly levelled at William Rufus – would be subjected to mutilation. Walter Map, writing later in the century, remarked: 'a market followed the king wherever he moved his camp'; everyone benefited. Henry retained several hundreds of knights, who were expected to be worthy of the wages and food that supported them. He insisted on his officials making fair payment for supplies requisitioned for the use of the royal household or for his soldiers. The way was open for men of humble origin (as the chronicler Orderic Vitalis noted) to become formidable in the service of the crown; a career open to talent became a reality. Among the outstanding lay officials in Henry's service were Richard Basset and Aubrey De Vere, who reformed the sheriffdoms of much of England.

Henry was especially fortunate in having Matilda as his queen, a capable woman respected for her piety, who acted as regent when Henry was in Normandy, where the king spent more than half his reign. Matilda had a keen interest in building projects and was very much an active partner to her husband.

The deaths of both Queen Matilda and Robert of Meulan in the same year (1118) must have come as a grievous blow to Henry. However, even these were overshadowed in November 1120 by the tragic loss of his heir William in the *White Ship* tragedy.

Channel crossings were never risk-free undertakings, especially when excessive alcohol (as reportedly here) was consumed. The vessel, newly refitted, struck a submerged rock near the Normandy coast off Barfleur. The *White Ship*, which claimed the lives of many well-connected young people, was a disaster of the first magnitude. Only one of approximately 300 people on board survived. Henry was personally devastated – and his plans for the succession and for a new dynasty were wrecked.

Henry's second marriage, to Adeliza of Louvain, was childless. For the remainder of the reign the succession remained deeply uncertain. William Clito, son of Robert Curthose (still in captivity), obviously had a strong claim, at least to Normandy; not unnaturally, he became a focus for those Normans opposed to his uncle's rule, and for some years it also suited the French king Louis VI ('the Fat') to take up his cause. Clito's death in 1128 must have come as a great relief to Henry. Given that there were no precedents for female succession in England or Normandy, the king had already taken out further insurance by betrothing his daughter Matilda – by now the widow of the German emperor – to Geoffrey, the son and heir of Fulk, count of Anjou. He needed to forge this alliance to prevent Anjou supporting rebels in Normandy. Matilda was also Henry's choice of successor. There remained, however, an unanswered question: Was the 'empress' (as Matilda preferred to style herself) to rule in her own right, and what part would her husband play? In fact it would prove to be the claims of the empress' son Henry (born 1133), not those of the lady herself, that the baronage would find acceptable.

Throughout his long reign Henry proved highly adept at maintaining the loyalty of much of his baronage. For those who were incorrigible rebels (pre-eminently Robert of Bellême) the penalties were imprisonment and forfeiture – nothing more drastic; others, such as Waleran of Meulan (Robert of Meulan's son) might in due season be restored to position and favour. But royal patronage was always unpredictable. The contemporary chronicler archdeacon Henry of Huntingdon described Henry as 'a man of the deepest dissimulation and inscrutability of mind.'

Henry's relations with the French king were, perforce, not easy. Louis initially supported (though he subsequently abandoned) William Clito's claims. Additionally, there was the matter of homage for Normandy: Henry, as duke, was a vassal of the French king, his overlord for that territory. Henry, cautious by instinct, preferred diplomacy to the sword. With France there was more than a decade of peace before the reign ended. The Welsh princes swore oaths of allegiance to him; Henry was satisfied if they submitted and paid tribute; and relative stability was maintained along the borders. Alexander I, king of Scotland, whose sister was Henry's queen, acknowledged Henry's overlordship and there was an unbroken peace. But for Henry it was the security of Normandy and its defence that was his constant preoccupation. The fact remained that he had no clear 'right' to the duchy. Men who rebelled there, some of whom (it is reported) were blinded, were betraying the king's trust. Such severity, perhaps more associated with Byzantine politics, was apparently not regarded as harsh by the standards of the time, likewise the castration of the moneyers for striking, it was alleged, lightweight coins ('my money' – Henry's characteristic voice!) was not deemed shocking.

Was Henry himself fully literate? We have on record the quip attributed to him: that an unlearned king was like a crowned ass. In later times historians awarded him the nickname 'Beauclerc' ('fine scholar'). None of this, however, is finally conclusive.

Orderic Vitalis called Henry the mightiest king ever to sit on the English throne. Both the contemporary scholar, William of Malmesbury, and the *Peterborough Chronicle* were deeply sympathetic to Henry, as was Walter Map: 'The court was a school of virtue and wisdom before dinner, after it a place of companionship and respectful mirth.' The judgement of Henry of Huntingdon was that Henry had three gifts: wisdom, victory and riches; these were however offset by three vices, those of avarice, cruelty and lust. The sin of avarice is a serious matter in all conscience, and Henry certainly was very rich indeed. As for the rest, the reader may be the judge.

CHAPTER 2

HENRY II (1154-1189)

Henry II

On 1 December 1135 Henry I died in Normandy from 'a surfeit of lampreys' (a jawless eel-like fish), so the chronicler, Henry of Huntingdon, relates. He was 67 years of age and at the height of his powers and fame, 'the father of his people' (to quote Walter Map). Even men who had bridled under Henry's strong rule would soon come to regret his passing.

The protagonists in the succession conflict were Henry's own choice of successor, his daughter Empress Matilda, widow of Emperor Henry V and now wife of Geoffrey of Anjou, and his nephew Stephen, count of Blois, whose mother was the Conqueror's daughter Adele. The empress' principal supporter was her half-brother Robert, earl of Gloucester, one of the late king's illegitimate offspring and a man of resolution and ability; she was, however, possessed of a certain haughtiness of demeanour which many found alienating. Stephen, though an affable and chivalrous knight, altogether lacked a capacity for steely governance – the parallel with Robert Curthose is inescapable; had Stephen been otherwise, he would most likely have prevailed in the ensuing conflict.

Stephen seized the initiative by crossing the Channel and was duly crowned in Westminster Abbey on 22 December. Henry I had extracted oaths of allegiance to the empress from the barons, many of whom now found it expedient to abandon their obligation towards her. The advantage in the succession of petty skirmishes and battles passed from one side to the other; neither was finally able to prevail. The period is widely called a time of 'anarchy': a time when 'Christ and his Saints slept', to quote the *Peterborough Chronicle*.

Eventually a compromise was brokered – in itself no mean achievement: Stephen would remain king during his lifetime; his successor would be Matilda and Geoffrey's son (born in 1133) who became Henry II in 1154; the empress herself, following the death of Earl Robert, had meanwhile given up the struggle and retired to Anjou.

* * *

The far-flung territories that Henry inherited were truly remarkable in scope. Apart from being 'king of the English', Henry was recognised as duke of Normandy, which his father Geoffrey had taken, and in 1151, on Geoffrey's death, he succeeded him as count of Anjou; then in 1152 he married Eleanor of Aquitaine, becoming additionally duke of Aquitaine. This 'Angevin Empire' – Henry and his successors were known as the Angevin kings because they were descended from Geoffrey, count of Anjou – might have seemed scarcely manageable, but Henry, aged 21, was a young man of prodigious energy as well as possessing high intelligence.

Henry II was a restless man, always on the move, bow-legged from riding, covering huge distances and leaving his grumbling companions trailing in his wake. He had to be on the move, for it was only Henry's person – and the point can scarcely be exaggerated – who brought unity to the empire. A passionate man, prone to outbreaks of anger (he lacked his grandfather's self-control), he comes across as intensely human. He was less calculating, more volatile but no less intelligent than his grandfather, whom he revered for his achievement in bringing order and good governance and who was his exemplar.

Henry fascinated his contemporaries, whether or not they liked him. As king he had no interest in ostentation or personal finery; his clothing was generally simple and functional. Certainly he was an accessible figure as he travelled the length and breadth of his dominions. Henry set himself and his servants very high standards; about such matters he was passionate.

Henry's hallmark energy and resolve were evident from the first year of his reign. Lands that had been granted by King Stephen to his supporters were reclaimed and their earldoms abolished. 'Adulterine' castles (those that had sprung up during the Anarchy without royal warrant) were dismantled. Henry only built one completely new castle himself: at Orford in Suffolk, to consolidate royal power in the region.

Henry's reign was profoundly constructive in many ways. Inevitably, however, the controversy with Thomas Becket with its tragic denouement has tended, at least in the public consciousness, to take centre stage.

Henry and Thomas Becket were boon companions in youth. Thomas had been a clerk in the household of Archbishop Theobald of Canterbury, with whom it seems the king had a cordial relationship. On Theobald's death in 1161, Henry secured the election of Thomas, already his chancellor and intimate in his counsels, to Canterbury. This was a time when – as we have seen with the Investiture Controversy – a self-confident papacy was asserting its claims vis-à-vis the secular power. Henry, with his keen intelligence, must have seen Thomas as the ideal collaborator in fostering a harmonious church-state relationship of his own choosing. Alas, he fatally misjudged his man.

Thomas Becket has never been short of detractors. How was the rather fashionable 'man about town' transformed into the austere, ascetic upholder of the Church's claims? None of this could have been anticipated. Still, it seems that Henry's mother, the empress, always available to advise from her Rouen retirement, had reservations about the appointment. Other clerics, far more experienced, must not unjustifiably have resented being passed over. Reasons of personal ambition apart, was not Thomas far too obviously 'the king's man'? And anyway wasn't Thomas far too 'worldly'? Widespread scepticism surely must have greeted the news of his advancement, certainly on the part of Gilbert Foliot, bishop of London, who opposed it.

On 2 June Thomas – remarkably not yet in holy orders – became a priest. The next day he was consecrated archbishop. Thereupon he resigned all his secular offices. He became a 'new man', confounding both his critics and the king himself. One may perhaps believe that Thomas, a complex and enigmatic person, wanted to convince the world and also himself that he was no time-serving prelate at hand to do the king's bidding. Henry, who could never abide disloyalty, was initially bewildered and later outraged by Becket's constant insistence on the Church's rights and the Church's law. As events unfolded, their personal relationship collapsed in bitterness and rancour. A number of Thomas' episcopal colleagues were in fact unsympathetic to him; some saw the quarrel as personal, not general. (One contemporary saw Thomas in a dream as a prickly hedgehog.)

There followed a series of minor disputes, leading to a major quarrel over the punishment of 'criminous clerks' (clergy convicted of a crime). Henry wanted a defrocked cleric to suffer the same punishment as a layman; the spiritual penances imposed by the Church were, in his view, insufficient and no deterrent. Thomas, however, was unflinching in his view that church courts alone had the authority to judge a cleric. In any case, was it just for a defrocked cleric to face penalties imposed at a further trial in a secular court? Was a man in minor orders entitled to claim 'benefit of clergy'? Pleading 'benefit of clergy' had become notorious.

The Constitutions of Clarendon (1164), reflecting the king's resolution to replace 'ancient customs' (not actually recorded) with a written version, led to a bitter argument. Becket, who would only give his verbal assent, called them 'pernicious innovations', contrary to canon law. The upshot was that in October 1164 Archbishop Thomas (like Archbishop Anselm before him) fled the country, not returning for six years. In the years that followed serious attempts were made to bridge the chasm that divided the two men; finally, though, these foundered due to a combination of pride and intransigence. The reality was that their relationship was irretrievably broken.

The ancient rivalry between the sees of Canterbury and York further exacerbated the conflict. Henry was anxious to have his eldest surviving son, also named Henry (thereafter known as 'the young king'), crowned in his own lifetime. By custom, anointing and crowning a new king was reserved to Canterbury but, in Thomas' absence, the pope had earlier authorised the archbishop of York to perform the act. Now in June 1170 Henry ordered York to carry out the ceremony. Thomas, with papal support, threatened an interdict (an order closing all the churches in the kingdom) and received authority also to excommunicate the bishops who had assisted at the coronation. This called into question the validity of the ceremony, and so undermined Henry's plans for the succession.

On 1 December 1170 Thomas, now clearly beyond compromise, returned to England. The sequel is well known: the murder of Thomas on the evening of Tuesday 29 December in his own cathedral by four knights, incited by the wrath contained in Henry's unguarded words uttered at his court at Argentan. Efforts, alas unavailing, were made to arrest their progress. Henry, in reality a sensitive man with a deep sense of personal responsibility, was utterly devastated, even traumatised, by this outcome. The shockwaves from this act of murder and sacrilege were felt across medieval Christendom; possibly no other event so profoundly shocked men's consciences.

As a penitential act of self-abasement, Henry consented to be scourged by the monks of Canterbury and the attending prelates (respectively, three and five strokes of the rod apiece). Then, after a night's public humiliation by the tomb, came what might seem miraculous events: King William the Lion of Scotland was captured by royal troops (he was finally released in 1174); a Flemish invasion fleet in the Channel was dispersed; and, soon enough, a major revolt by Henry's own sons collapsed. King William would subsequently be required to do homage for his kingdom, and all his vassals had to swear loyalty to Henry. From his grave the soon-to-be saint – canonisation duly followed in March 1173 – could be seen as acting for his now fully shriven old friend.

*   *   *

Henry's relationship with his wife, the celebrated Eleanor, whom he married at the age of 19 (she was 10 years his senior) within weeks of her divorce from King Louis VII of France, must have been tempestuous at times, especially when the queen took the part of her sons against their father. Fiery, bold and resourceful, she was never prepared to live in her husband's shadow. Eleanor bore Henry eight children, all but one of whom survived to adulthood. Henry's relationship with his wayward sons was, to put it mildly, deeply problematic. Yet whenever they rebelled, his constant wish was for reconciliation.

At the heart of the problem lay the sheer geographical reach of the Angevin Empire: essentially ungovernable by one man, even one as energetic and able as Henry. The solution, sensible enough in principle, might seem to lie in devolving significant responsibilities to his sons; hence, in part, the coronation of 'the young king' (he proved disloyal to his father and died aged only 26 in 1183). The practice, however, was a failure. Henry was not minded to cede serious power to anyone; his sons, themselves in contact with the French court, grew restive and rebelled. Then there were other 'players' in the background: the mother Eleanor, commonly apart from her husband, taking her sons' side, and, especially, the French kings, Louis VII and his wily son Philip, seeking to derive maximum benefit from the feuding family.

Henry was deeply knowledgeable about the law – his counsel was widely sought – and had a passion above all, following the period of 'anarchy', for justice, law, order and good government. The king was an activist: he heard cases and also gave judgement. The glory of Henry's reign lies in the foundation of English 'common' law (the law which applied throughout the land), in which his justiciar, Ranulf de Glanvil, was a key figure. Henry developed the system of circuit judges (the king was personally involved in their selection), who heard both civil and criminal cases in a group of 'counties'. Written records were maintained. Juries, comprising 12 knights and freemen from each hundred – a subdivision of a county or shire, rooted in the Saxon past – were made part of the king's justice; here can be found the origin of the modern jury system. Henry was angered by corrupt sheriffs (the officials in charge of counties), many of whom were removed from office. Sheriffs took on their roles as tax collectors on the basis that they paid a fixed sum to the exchequer and then collected as much tax as they were entitled to in order to cover that sum: an arrangement clearly open to abuse.

In addition Henry established a number of 'assizes' to address the problem of a strong man seizing his neighbour's land; this reinforced the notion that the royal court was the fount of justice and a normal place in which to settle even relatively minor disputes. In his determination to secure order and justice Henry sought the advice of some of the best educated men in the kingdom (as at the councils at Clarendon, 1163 and 1166). He was a practical man rather than an innovator; starting from his grandfather's laws and institutions he had a fierce eagerness to find the best ways of making things work.

The practical legacy of the Becket calamity – aside from the pressing need to fill the many vacancies (only Canterbury itself was to be filled by a monk, others went to royal servants) – had consequences perhaps less far-reaching than might be supposed. The Constitutions of Clarendon, inevitably, were abrogated but many of the clauses stayed quietly in effect. Politics being a practical business, compromises and new ways of working had to be found. In 1176 the king accepted that 'criminous clerks', having lost their status, should not face a secular trial: a hardening of Rome's stance, and an endorsement of Becket's. But Henry kept control over what mattered to him most: appointments and vacancies.

In Henry's absence on the continent – he spent only 37% of his reign in Britain – Eleanor headed the English government, though as the years passed, she was increasingly overseas, holding her own court in Anjou. Robert, earl of Leicester, Richard de Lucy, Henry's justiciars, and Richard Fitz Nigel, the treasurer (and nephew of Henry I's great bishop Roger), were pre-eminent among the expert and long-serving servants upon whom the king depended absolutely; they acted as regents in the king's absence, chief ministers when he was present. One of Henry's first acts was the re-organisation of the administration and national finances. The unbroken series of fiscal records, the Pipe Rolls, now begins.

In Ireland Henry, early in his reign, obtained a grant from the pope making him its Lord. Most of the southern 'kings' (essentially tribal leaders) did homage to him. Richard de Clare, earl of Pembroke, an important Welsh lord, posed a potential threat: as guardian of the borders of Wales (the 'marches') he was making alliances with various Irish 'kings'. Henry acted decisively: he crossed to Ireland in late 1171 with a powerful army. Ulster remained fiercely independent and Henry made no attempt to subjugate its 'kings'. In Wales Henry strengthened his alliances and lordship over the native rulers.

The year 1180 was decisive for the prospects of the Angevin Empire. Across the Channel Louis VII was succeeded by his son Philip II: determined, ambitious, an expansionist and the master-schemer of his age, the new king – the first to style himself 'King of France' – was in the course of time to prove a far more formidable adversary than his father. That said, Louis VII also showed considerable acumen in exploiting Henry's family feuds.

'The young king', denied of any real power, made common cause with Louis (his father-in-law), though his rebellion in 1173, involving also Henry's sons, Richard and Geoffrey, was quashed (just when Henry was doing his penance). Philip assiduously cultivated Richard, who was now heir to the throne and, unlike 'the young king', already a renowned warrior. At the very end Philip and Richard in combination brought the great king, now seriously ill, to his knees: an ignominious end to a reign touched with genuine greatness. The desertion of Henry's youngest son John must have been the bitterest blow of all.

Henry's weaknesses were his uncontrollable outbursts of temper (how the memory of Becket must have haunted him all his days!) and – arguably – his refusal to contemplate any meaningful power-sharing with his sons, which poisoned their relationship. But this is debatable. Without Henry's tight control the sheer scope of the Angevin Empire made effective rule an impossibility. There is anyway a great deal more to be said on the positive side: the restoration of order and – certainly by any meaningful contemporary comparisons – the establishment of good governance; his shrewd choice of able servants and the trust he placed in them and, above all, his passion for justice and his huge personal involvement in the development of the common law.

It is notable that for all the intensity of the family strife, above all in the crisis years of 1173-4, following which Queen Eleanor, who had aided and abetted her sons, suffered a lengthy period of imprisonment, and also in 1183, Henry treated all the rebels with a degree of forbearance – certainly no executions followed. It was around the time of Eleanor's imprisonment that Henry's liaison with the young noblewoman Rosamund Clifford ('The Fair Rosamund' of romantic myth) became common knowledge. At heart, certainly where his family was concerned, he was a deeply emotional man; this is in stark contrast to his almost severely rational approach to governance.

Many chroniclers expressed immense admiration for Henry. William of Newburgh commented: 'He abhorred bloodshed and the sacrifice of men's lives, and strove diligently to keep the peace'; in this regard he was successful, at least in England, the invasion of 1173 excepted. 'He was liberal beyond compare in alms-giving', wrote Gerald of Wales (not an uncritical admirer); and he opened his storehouses in the face of famine in Anjou and Maine. In contrast his personal outlay was quite modest. Walter Map, courtier and writer, praised his lack of pride: 'he does not magnify himself as more than man.' Ralph Diss, dean of St Paul's, saw him as 'the father of the English': an accolade already awarded by Walter Map to Henry's grandfather. Underpinning everything was Henry's real sense of care for his kingdom. Of all the kings under review here he has some claim to be regarded as the most sympathetic in human terms.

The Angevin Empire, however, was to prove ephemeral, and the king himself was the only unifying factor linking its far-flung lands. Within two decades of Henry's death, Philip II (now styled 'Augustus') had regained all of Normandy, Brittany and much of Aquitaine for the French crown.

CHAPTER 3

HENRY III (1216-1272)

Henry III

Henry III was the elder son of the notorious King John (1199-1216). He was crowned as a boy of nine and his reign lasted 56 years, the longest in English medieval history. It may then seem surprising that, in public awareness, this Henry is rather overlooked; even as we must acknowledge that he was hardly the most energetic or politically astute of his line. Yet the reign was deeply significant: for the origins of parliament above all, and also for the rebuilding of Westminster Abbey. It really falls into two parts: up to 1258, the time of Henry's largely untrammelled personal rule; and the period after, when more dominating figures took centre stage.

*   *   *

King John died of dysentery at Newark on 18 October 1216 and was buried, as he had wished, in Worcester Cathedral, where he still rests. His elder brother Richard I (the 'Lionheart'), king 1189-1199, had proved a worthy antagonist and rival to the French king, Philip Augustus (so called because he 'augmented' the territory of the royal domain). John was not a man of like mettle. His reign was both disastrous and momentous.

In 1216 the French king's son Louis, offered the throne by John's rebellious barons, controlled more than half of England. John had by then lost Normandy (in 1204, clearly a watershed moment) and Anjou. The barons had forced him to concede Magna Carta (Great Charter), to which John granted his seal in June 1215, which placed unprecedented limits on kingship.

Magna Carta was in the form of a royal grant to all free men in perpetuity. John pledged himself and his successors not to abuse the overlord's right to have custody of minor heirs, to levy inheritance payments, to arrange the marriages of minor heirs, heiresses and widows. The burden represented by the royal forest would be lightened; its bounds and administration were for the first time regulated. Taxes known as 'scutage' (a tax paid in lieu of military service on the lands of the nobility) and 'aids' ('voluntary' payments made to support the king in special enterprises or to supplement scutage to fund his military projects) would not be levied without 'the common counsel of the kingdom'. Royal justice – now the favoured first resort – would be more equitable and accessible. The Church was promised liberty.

'No free man shall be seized, imprisoned, dispossessed,
outlawed, exiled or ruined in any way, nor shall we attack him
or send men to attack him, except by the lawful judgment of
his peers and the law of the land. To no one will we sell, to no
one will we deny or delay right of justice.'
(Magna Carta clauses 39 and 40)

Perhaps most remarkable was the 'security clause', setting up a
committee of 25 barons to ensure that the monarch and his
servants complied with the terms of the Charter.

John hoped that the Charter, having brought peace and the
restoration of his authority, would essentially be toothless. The barons
saw things quite differently and expected rigorous enforcement. John's
personality – his perceived ruthless and arbitrary rule – had provoked
hostility and fear. Many grievances had a distinctly personal hue.
There had been a great quarrel between the king and Pope Innocent
III over the election of a new archbishop of Canterbury. The
imposition of a papal interdict (the suspension of church services,
from 1208 to 1214) on England might be seen as justifying rebellion
against an unholy king. John had been excommunicated. His raising
of taxes, in a failed attempt to recover his continental lands, had
aroused anger and affected everyone, the baronage being especially
resentful. Justice was at the same time sold and denied.

John's decisive defeat at Bouvines (1214) shattered his authority.
It led directly to the celebrated meeting at Runnymede, the great
meadow beside the Thames, where Magna Carta was hammered
out in negotiations. Archbishop Stephen Langton of Canterbury,
a mediator between the two sides, but fundamentally in sympathy
with baronial aims, was heavily involved in the drafting and
securing of Magna Carta. When Pope Innocent III subsequently
annulled the Charter (on the basis that its terms had been

extracted by force, and as such were not legally binding), the rebels renounced their homage to John – hence their invitation to Prince Louis to invade. Civil war now raged.

*   *   *

Henry III was crowned at Gloucester Abbey on 28 October 1216 – just 10 days after his father's death. John's deathbed thoughts, apart from concern for his own soul, were centred on the future of his dynasty. He appealed to the executors of his will and to the new pope, Honorius III for his sons' protection. It was entirely appropriate for the pope to be the boy-king's legal guardian: John had earlier 'given' the kingdom of England to the pope, as feudal overlord above the king, receiving it back as a papal fief. The papal legate Cardinal Guala was granted the fullest powers and he oversaw the child's coronation. Speed was of the essence, for there was a rival claimant to the throne: Louis of France. But now Henry was an anointed king and the regime had thereby gained legitimacy.

Who would lead the government? One man alone had the required gravitas: William Marshal, earl of Pembroke, the renowned (now septuagenarian) knight, a loyal and respected servant of the crown going back to Henry II's time. Hubert de Burgh, holder of the office of justiciar (second only to the king), was the other key figure and also the hero of the hour having, as castellan of Dover Castle, repulsed Louis' siege engines. Dover was crucial: it was aptly called 'the key to England'. In September 1217 Louis was persuaded to leave England.

A royal minority in England was bound to be problematic – the last one, involving Æthelred (the Unready), had been well over 200 years earlier. In 1218 the council prudently decided to create a Great Seal for Henry; his government was now issuing orders with his authority. Marshal, becoming in effect regent, was personally devoted to Henry; he would never, he said, desert the boy, even if it meant carrying him on his shoulders from country to country, begging for bread.

After William Marshal's death (1219), government was in the hands of Pandulf, the new papal legate, acting with the justiciar Hubert de Burgh and the royal tutor Peter des Roches, bishop of Winchester, both of whom had stood loyal to John. In May 1220 a second coronation of Henry was organised, this time in the proper place (Westminster Abbey) and presided over by the right man (the archbishop of Canterbury, Stephen Langton). At the end of 1223 Henry, now aged 16, took custody of the Great Seal and thereafter he attested all matters of importance.

The relationship between Hubert and Bishop Peter, the king's guardian, was an uneasy one. Until 1232 Hubert, a man of great political acumen who had the backing of Archbishop Langton (until his death in 1228), dominated the scene. It was he above all who taught Henry the business of government, though the experience of later events may leave it open to question how much Henry had actually learnt. In that year Peter, his reputation having been enhanced by going on crusade, displaced Hubert. In 1234 Henry, responding to pressure, dismissed Peter and took personal charge of his kingdom. All things considered though, the leading ministers had done a remarkable job in restoring the crown's position and its finances. There now followed a period when solid, responsible government was in short supply.

John's death and Henry's accession gave Magna Carta a new lease of life. In February 1225 Henry issued new versions of Magna Carta and the Charter of the Forest. These Charters, the final reconciliation after the civil wars, were the first to be authenticated with Henry III's seal. They became definitive, having the status of law. They were a watershed moment in English government. Later kings simply confirmed the clauses of 1225. Magna Carta's lasting contribution lay in its insistence that even a king had to respect the common law. The community of the realm (the 'common counsel') now had to be asked directly in a great council or a 'parlement' (from the French 'parler', to speak) before new taxes were imposed. This was a crucial development.

The backdrop was the king's bid to retain Gascony (successful, as it turned out), which required money raised through the levying of a tax of a fifteenth on moveable goods. The magnates granted Henry this taxation in return for the reissue of Magna Carta and the Charter of the Forest. Now the contract was granted to 'all of our realm', not just to 'all the free men and women of our realm'. What was missing, however, was the security clause of 1215, which had empowered 25 barons to enforce the Charter. There was, as a result, no constitutional means of enforcing the Charter.

Henry's personality was in many ways attractive: warm-hearted, generous and instinctively conciliatory and, unlike his father John, he was not in the least personally vicious. Whether he was well suited to face the challenges of medieval kingship is quite another matter!

The king, whose confessors were drawn from the Dominican friars, was always a dutiful son of the pope. His deep personal piety was at the heart of his being, and was manifested above all in the rebuilding of Edward the Confessor's Abbey at Westminster; Henry was devoted to the Confessor's cult and named his eldest son Edward after the final legitimate Anglo-Saxon ruler. He took an informed interest in the Abbey's redevelopment, spending in the order of £50,000, a prodigious sum; he regarded it as both his and his dynasty's mausoleum. Up to 400 men were employed on the project at any one time. Matthew Paris, a Benedictine monk at St Albans Abbey, and the most celebrated chronicler of the age, called the building 'incomparable'. The king fed 500 paupers a day and washed the feet of the poor. Henry probably viewed himself as a confessor of the faith rather than a martyr. Despite lacking any personal martial capability, he had hopes of going on crusade – probably mindful of his exact contemporary Louis IX's example ('St Louis' as he became) – and in 1250 went so far as to take the cross, perhaps best seen as a rather naïve statement of intent. He placed great emphasis on the sanctity of his kingship.

Henry's fervent wish for the conversion of the Jews, seen as the killers of Christ – that leitmotif running through European history, often with the most tragic consequences – may be viewed as an offshoot of his piety. Extortionate levies were imposed on the Jewish communities, their wealth broken by taxation. A 'domus conversorum' was established to house Jews who chose to convert.

Henry, basically a pacific individual, was probably happiest when visiting (and often embellishing) his palaces and places of religion – of which he was a generous benefactor – mainly in southern England. A contemporary chronicler called him *'simplex'*: the meaning – guileless, straightforward, or possibly stupid – itself is rather ambiguous. It is significant that this description was applied from early in the reign. Certainly he was easily influenced, too easily led, and his excessive generosity – especially to a large network of relatives, many of them foreigners – would in time become the source of many of his problems and would excite intense hostility.

Henry must have been acutely conscious of the looming presence of Magna Carta as he entered upon the full responsibilities of kingship. In practice, despite hints of greater assertiveness, his style of kingship was not aggressive after the manner of his father or his own son Edward. By and large he acted within the terms of the Charter, which he confirmed in 1237 and 1253. That said, according to Matthew Paris, in 1252 he claimed that he could set aside at will previously granted charters.

In January 1236 Henry married Eleanor of Provence, aged 12, from the House of Savoy, a powerful dynasty of southern Europe. The Savoyard affinity thereafter became central to the political establishment. Henry, characteristically, rewarded them generously. Much later Eleanor would prove an invaluable political player, and a great deal tougher than her husband.

Henry's mother, Isabella of Angoulême, had returned home the year after King John's death and was now married to Hugh de Lusignan, head of the dominant family in the county of Poitou. Henry planned to recover Poitou (lost by his father). However, the French king Louis IX, himself married to Queen Eleanor's sister, wanted to invest his own brother as count there. In 1242 Henry failed to persuade parliament to grant him the necessary aid to fund his campaign. Instead he had to undertake it with his own resources. The mission was a fiasco and in September 1243 Henry, his reputation tarnished, returned to England.

Henry promoted and supported generously his mother's new family, his Lusignan half-brothers, and their followers, who now, at the king's invitation, also descended upon the court. The influx of 'aliens' and the largesse that came their way (offices, favourable marriages, lands) provoked intense hostility, notably from Matthew Paris, who was himself acquainted with the king. Matthew's intense dislike of foreigners (in another age the authentic 'Brexit Spirit') and the 'alien' colonisation of the court and its circles may have been widely shared. To make matters worse, the two networks were often mutually hostile. Henry's patronage of his half-brothers created a faction that began to rival the Savoyards. His unwillingness, or his inability, to control these competing court factions was a crucial weakness in his governance.

Simon de Montfort, who would become the baronial leader in the greatest conflict of the reign, is a controversial figure. The younger son of a French noble, he arrived in England in 1230 to advance his claim to the earldom of Leicester. He and Henry were brothers-in-law, Simon having married the king's sister Eleanor. Their relationship was a complicated one. Religious zeal was a vital force in Simon's motivation, and his own father had led a crusade. His idealism was influenced by contact with leading churchmen and the example of Louis IX of France ('St Louis'). The barons, in his view, had a vocation to reform the realm in order to purge their own souls. With his huge self-confidence and charisma, Simon was a natural leader, albeit (as events played out) a divisive one. Henry's religiosity, apart from an open-handed generosity to the poor and afflicted, was centred on the Abbey project and peregrinations to religious houses. The brothers-in-law could scarcely have been more different! Simon was everything that Henry wasn't: a charismatic leader with strong military credentials.

In 1248 Henry appointed Simon as his lieutenant in Gascony, then in a state of great disorder, but resentment at Simon's high-handed and harsh methods, ravaging his enemies' lands, led to his recall. On trial at Westminster he brilliantly defended himself against all charges and was duly acquitted. King and earl exchanged bitter words. Henry, probably a nervous man, was much later reported as saying that he feared Simon 'more than all the thunder and lightning in the world'.

If Earl Simon made Henry fearful, the pope attracted his unqualified devotion. Probably Henry always felt he owed his succession, to a large extent, to the pope and his legates; otherwise the civil war might well have dragged on and Prince Louis might not have agreed to leave so soon. His dedication to the interests of the papacy – probably vying with his brother king Louis IX across the Channel – led in part to the great crisis of 1258.

Henry schemed to secure the Sicilian throne for his younger son Edmund (Edward, the elder, had already been granted Gascony).

The papacy was seeking a champion to take on its enemy, the Hohenstaufen dynasty, in southern Italy and Sicily. The terms – raising and transporting an army to Italy, paying the papacy annual tribute and £90,000 to reimburse its expenses, and providing knights for the papal army – were greeted with predictable disbelief and outrage when announced in parliament (October 1255). The magnates absolutely refused to grant a tax. Matthew Paris' condemnation of Henry's actions was severe. He also denounced the pope for the demands he had placed on Henry. The king had been, it was widely believed, led astray by 'foreigners'. The barons' case was that they were the king's 'natural' advisers, that their role had been usurped by Henry's foreign friends and relatives, who acted as though they were above the law.

*   *   *

Parliament reconvened at Oxford in June 1258. The Provisions of Oxford established a new system of government that would create an alliance to drive forward the 'reform of the realm and to redress the state of the realm'. A new Council of Fifteen was established, comprising seven earls, five barons, the archbishop of Canterbury, the bishop of Worcester, and one royal clerk. The three great officers of state, justiciar, chancellor, and treasurer, were to be appointed by and responsible to this council. Parliament should meet, it was determined, three times a year: in October, February and June. Attempts were also made to curb abuses of power in the localities: four knights were appointed in each county to investigate wrongs allegedly committed by the king's officers. Hugh Bigod, the justiciar, showed impressive energy and his services were much in demand; a great number of people thought that they had been victims of a miscarriage of justice. The Provisions of Oxford, supplemented by the Provisions of

Westminster (1259), formed the basis of English government until 1262 and proved to be widely popular. The king was reduced to being a mere cypher in his own realm.

In late 1259 the Treaty of Paris between England and France was ratified. This marked the formal end of the Angevin Empire. By its terms Henry renounced all claims to the continental lands lost by his father. As for Aquitaine, he acknowledged that he held it 'from the kingdom of France', for which he was therefore required to perform homage in person. Clearly Henry, who always aspired to be a significant player on the international stage, gave up a great deal. But at least peace with France would enable him to pursue his cherished plan to take Sicily.

In December Simon de Montfort, pre-eminent in the Council of Fifteen and so a key figure in the negotiations leading to the treaty, returned to England without taking leave of the king, who was then in France. It was suspected by Henry that his heir Edward, himself opposed to the treaty's terms, might be seeking an accord with Earl Simon, possibly even to usurp the throne; both had an interest in wanting to see royal government effective. Henry's overextended stay in France (attributed to serious illness) led to harsh words from his host: King Louis reproached him for the 'shame' and 'harm' that his absence from England was causing. Probably stung by his brother-in-law's stern words, the newly energised Henry ordered the justiciar to prepare for his return, banned the meetings of parliament, and summoned the feudal levy to muster at London. He denounced Simon to the baronage and declared his intention to rule again as supreme. Edward, unaccustomed to his father's new-found assertiveness, submitted. Facing trial for his actions, Simon once again brilliantly acquitted himself of any hint of disloyalty, won back the support of many of his peers and, by dint of his extraordinary charisma, regained his ascendency over the king.

In this fast-moving and fluid situation Henry appealed to the pope, who duly obliged by quashing the Provisions of Oxford; additionally, he enjoined full obedience to the royal will upon all Henry's subjects. In February 1261 Henry fled to the Tower of London, renowned for its impregnability, accusing the council of usurping his position. His Lusignan relatives now began to return to England and resume their accustomed roles. Henry replaced the baronial appointments of justiciar, chancellor and treasurer with his own men. With Edward clearly now onside the king was intent on taking the conflict to his barons. He replaced all the sheriffs appointed by the council with his own men. At this point Simon went into exile in France, preferring to 'die landless than depart from the truth and be perjured'. Henry, apparently secure in his triumph, could now return to his old obsession, the Sicilian affair.

Nonetheless, the Provisions of Oxford and the reforms brought about in its wake had aroused expectations, going down the social order, that there did exist a 'community of our realm' and that grievances should be redressed. The baronial agenda had acquired a more popular resonance.

Henry imprudently now left for France, probably seeking to undermine Simon de Montfort's position at court there. People were ignorant, wrote the Dunstable chronicler, of the reason for his journey and many 'took fright regarding the future'. He stayed a full five months (July to December 1262), leaving a vacuum at the heart of his government: an extraordinary dereliction of duty. Disaffection mounted and, in Wales, rebellion was brewing.

Simon had meanwhile returned to England and in October 1262 read out to parliament a Bull from the new pope, Urban IV, confirming the Provisions of Oxford and revoking the king's absolution from his oath to abide by them.

In July 1263, following a successful rebellion mounted by Simon and his allies (Welsh, Londoners, baronial rebels), a peace was announced: the Provisions of Oxford were reasserted and the call went up for all foreigners to be excluded from the government of England. Louis IX arbitrated at a remarkable meeting involving Simon, Henry, Queen Eleanor and their two sons. Each side agreed to be bound by the French king's judgement. It seems that Eleanor intervened to decisive effect – she was the sister of Louis' wife – and the French king unsurprisingly took Henry's part, 'quashing and invalidating' the Provisions; no subject could place limitations on Henry's rule. The king, Louis' argument ran, was entirely within his rights to declare the Provisions void while stating that Magna Carta stood. This view was not acceptable to Simon and his associates (and, it would seem, others besides), who formally renounced their homage to Henry.

Civil war began in February 1264 and culminated in the battle of Lewes in May: a set piece battle, one of those rare events in medieval England. Henry III, his brother Richard, earl of Cornwall, and the other loyalists were defeated; Edward and his cousin were to be held as hostages for the king's good behaviour.

From May 1264 to August 1265 Simon de Montfort was the effective ruler of the realm. A new conciliar form of government was established, comprising a group of three (Simon himself, the earl of Gloucester, and the bishop of Chichester) who would choose nine councillors. The scheme was in accord with the principles of the Provisions of Oxford. Though the king had no effective role in government, Simon kept him and Edward in his company. Simon's parliament of January 1265 was the first to which both knights and burgesses from the towns were summoned, leading it to be seen, in retrospect, as the first true parliament.

Meanwhile the baronial party was becoming increasingly fractured. Simon was widely seen as grasping and acquisitive, intent above all on the promotion of his own and his family's interests and amassing a fortune at others' expense. Some saw him as an extremist, self-righteous, arrogant and domineering; certainly he found collaboration difficult. At the same time he had huge numbers of devoted followers from a wide social spectrum. The defection from Simon's cause of the earl of Gloucester, who controlled the Welsh Marches, was crucial. Edward made a successful dash for freedom and came to terms with Gloucester.

The battle of Evesham (August 1265) was decisive: a coda of unprecedented brutality to the intense civil strife. Edward – never a man for half measures – and his associates formed an assassination squad to 'take out' Simon. All pretence at chivalric convention was abandoned. Simon's body – perhaps he was also seen as a traitor to his class – was shamefully mutilated. About 30 of Simon's leading supporters were deliberately done to death on the battlefield. The chronicler, Robert of Gloucester, called it 'the murder of Evesham, for battle it was none'. In death many revered Simon as a saint.

The war continued for two years after Evesham. If Henry and Edward had genuinely desired some form of reconciliation, the decision to confiscate the estates of the Montfortians achieved precisely the opposite result; and the principal beneficiaries were members of the royal family. The dowers of the widows of Evesham were also deemed forfeit. The Londoners, often prominent among Simon's supporters and especially effective at Lewes, were subjected to a huge fine. As a result, many of the rebels, having nothing to lose, decided to fight on.

The Dictum of Kenilworth (October 1266), a firm but moderate document, established the principle that former rebels could buy back their lands for a price that varied according to their involvement in the rebellion. In 1267 Henry promulgated the highly significant Statute of Marlborough, which enshrined in law the principle of title to land: men and women might hold their properties without punitive action on the part of the crown and rebels might be allowed to redeem their lands, though often it was at a crippling price.

Now Edward desired to join St Louis' crusade to the east. Henry was eventually able to persuade parliament to grant a twentieth on moveables. As a concomitant he was required to make concessions to the knights of the shire and the burgesses, including a restatement of the importance of the Charters of Liberties. Many of the ideas that had driven the baronial movement did not die at Evesham. Whilst initiative in government was restored to the king, parliament's pre-eminent position in the business of the realm was confirmed.

Henry's personal piety, his defining quality, was widely respected. A final assessment of his long reign, however, presents difficulties. The degree of his own commitment to Magna Carta, and what it represented, is questionable. His style of kingship diverged significantly from contemporary expectations. He was not the sort of king whom the English barons instinctively admired or even trusted. He was not a strong ruler, and most certainly not a military leader. He was prone to major errors of judgement: the imprudent and deeply resented largesse he distributed to his networks of relatives, their affinities and hangers-on; and his rather strange and deep-rooted obsession with the Sicilian affair. He was fortunate in having in his son Edward a confident, forceful and militarily able successor to buttress his position in his later years. His spouse, Eleanor of Provence, was made of far tougher stuff than the king and became a vital force in politics. His younger brother Richard, earl of Cornwall, who just predeceased Henry, was a capable, realistic and respected figure.

To Henry's credit are the long years of peace that his reign brought, combined with good relations with France, Scotland and finally with Wales. The population was growing, the country by and large becoming more prosperous. And, for the future, the notion of the 'community of the realm' was gathering force.

Henry III died in November 1272 when his son Edward was on crusade. It is indicative of the peace and good order now prevailing that Edward saw no compelling need to return to England until almost two years later.

CHAPTER 4

BRIDGE-PASSAGE:
THE FOURTEENTH CENTURY

The fourteenth was a century bereft of kings called Henry (until, that is, 1399 when Henry IV succeeded). It was a time for Edwards (named in homage to Edward the Confessor, king 1042-1066) and one Richard. All round it proved catastrophic.

Centuries sometimes can seem to come in pairs. Take the nineteenth, broadly progressive: industrialisation – a terrible, uprooting experience for many but finally leading to greater prosperity, the beginnings of public health reforms and the concerted fight against disease, the coming of the railways, movements towards universal education, a growing sense that children need protection and, above all, a time largely of peace; the lifespan, 1800-1894, of the hymnwriter Matthew Bridges feels optimal. (Victorian hymnwriters more generally may be seen as reflecting the expansive, optimistic mood of that era.) Now compare the twentieth century, certainly the first half: utter disaster, unspeakable barbarism and genocide.

Take now the thirteenth and fourteenth centuries. Across Europe the population had roughly doubled between 1000 and 1300 to perhaps close on 80 million. Many regions of Europe would not be this populated again until 1700. In England the population rose from perhaps 1.5 million to possibly 4 million.

The margin of error in such estimates is, however, very great. How does one explain this remarkable growth? For one thing the climate by and large – though there were, of course, terrible years – appears to have been relatively benign: this period, roughly from 900 to 1300, is spoken of as the Medieval Warm Period. Climate is essential: everything, lives and livelihoods, survival itself, depended on the quality of the harvest. Population growth fostered economic growth, networks of trade and markets, the development of towns and villages (some of them new). A transition from two-field to three-field agriculture, the increased use of horses for ploughing (a new horse collar was invented), iron production for tools and ploughs and the clearing of forested lands for cultivation (a process known as assarting) are some of the developments that have been identified in the period up to the 1300s as significant.

Soon after 1300 disaster struck: the Great Famine from 1315 to 1317. This was precipitated by alarming climate change: prolonged rain and very severe winters. There followed a decline in grain production and crop yields of perhaps an average of a third. Huge numbers of animals died from pestilence (murrains, animal plagues, were especially contagious). Probably 10-15% of the population either starved or experienced severe malnutrition, and of course the poor (the landless and hard-pressed smallholders) suffered disproportionately.

A generation later came the bubonic plague pandemic known to us as the Black Death and, to contemporaries, as the 'Great Mortality': an infinitely worse disaster, certainly the greatest that has befallen western Europe in the last 1,000 years. Its initial sweep through Europe from 1347 to 1351 was to be followed by frequent recurrences. In England between 1348 and 1485 there were 31 major outbreaks and localised occurrences continued into the seventeenth century. It was probably not until the 1470s that the population started rising again, perhaps reaching 3 million by the mid-16th century; thereafter, with a few setbacks, it rose steadily and sometimes dramatically.

These years were truly horrific and claimed the lives of upwards of 25 million people in Europe (estimates vary), between a third and a half of the population. Massive disorientation resulted. Cities, towns and hamlets were impoverished and in some cases left uninhabited. The death of so many labourers caused a drastic reduction in the amount of land under cultivation. In England demand for food fell, bringing prices down, but the acute scarcity of labour pushed wages up; in parliament legislation was passed (1349, 1351) to try to keep wages down to pre-plague levels.

People, great and small, must have been acutely conscious of the threats of recurring famine, plague and (rather later) the sweating sickness, not to mention intermittent warfare and more localised disorder; the supposedly masterful Henry VIII was always terrified of outbreaks. The last famine, thus far, in England was in 1596-7, following four disastrous harvests; the causes as before were incessant rain and unseasonable cold.

What had caused this unimaginable calamity? Why were God's people suffering? The global conflicts of more recent times have given rise to similar questioning. There were those who attributed the catastrophic epidemic to the conjunction of Saturn, Jupiter and Mars. But to the fourteenth-century mindset one fact must have seemed clear enough to many: God was angry. As in the years of the Great Famine, He was punishing people for their sins, their own, their community's, and the Church's (monks, living in close proximity, seem to have been disproportionately affected). How then to appease His wrath? Prayer, penitential psalms, processions, certainly – but was this of itself sufficient?

In Germany the Black Death precipitated in 1348/9 the greatest flagellant movement of all time; troupes of as many as 500 people, lashing themselves as a penitential act, moved through the countryside and into the towns. Some amongst these zealots may have believed themselves to be harbingers of a new Age of the Spirit foretold by the revelations of the abbot and hermit Joachim of Fiore (though this Age had been postulated for about 1260). Tragically, pogroms would sometimes be unleashed in their wake. The Jews, seen as responsible for the death of Christ, suffered horrendous acts of violence. In England, for whatever reason – official discouragement, possibly that English 'native reserve' – the flagellant movement found few, if any, followers. The Jews, who had suffered appallingly from pogroms in twelfth-century England, had been expelled by Edward I in 1290.

*　*　*

It is clear then that the English political elite was set to face unprecedented and unforeseen challenges within a few years of the fourteenth century dawning.

Edward I (1272-1307) was already a highly-experienced politician and warrior when he inherited from his father Henry III. His energy and resolution had been amply tested in the late travails of his father's reign, and they were never found to be wanting. A formidable and autocratic figure, he proved to be a great legislator and his reign was significant in parliament's development. The Edwardian conquest of Wales was a grim business; Scotland, however, survived. Political executions, for so long in abeyance, started up again, setting a precedent in their savagery for the years to come.

Edward II (1307-1327) – such a contrast to his father! – proved ineffectual and divisive. He had another tilt at the Scots and almost got killed at Bannockburn (1314). He was fatally susceptible to the influence of 'favourites' of questionable character, leading to the disintegration of his relationship with the nobility, his 'natural' counsellors. There followed an orgy of violence and politically motivated killings. The polity was deeply fractured. It all ended with the deposition and murder of the king himself.

His son Edward III (1327-1377) was a man of quite different mettle. Broadly speaking he was a skilful and pragmatic ruler, brave and chivalrous (the Knights of the Garter, which included the king himself, was his creation), who brought the nobility back into a working partnership. It is remarkable that his reign brought a high degree of domestic political stability, especially notable at the time of the Black Death and its aftermath. His late dalliance with Alice Perrers, though it may be viewed with indulgence, brought him no credit politically – quite the contrary. More to the point, the intermittent armed conflicts known as the Hundred Years War (1337-1453), originating from disputed claims to the succession to the French crown, started up in his day, and in the end there would be nothing to show for it; the English would be finally expelled, with only their Calais toehold remaining (finally lost in 1558). Repeated English invasions were organised on the pretext that its kings had a right to the French throne. It may be said that war, which was the nobility's ideal profession (as it still was in Henry VIII's time), played an important role in the growth of English nationalism. For the French this was an utterly dreadful experience involving the whole community. Vast swathes of the entire country were burnt and looted, the destruction exacerbated by French factional fighting.

Edward's son, Edward, the Black Prince, a feared and renowned warrior, predeceased (in 1376) his father. This left the throne to his nine-year-old son Richard II, a tragic and controversial figure, by no means lacking in personal courage (his conduct during the 'Peasants' Revolt' of 1381 bears this out). Finally, a tendency towards autocracy, combined with poor political judgement, led to his demise. Still, to his credit, Richard negotiated a truce with France. His supplanter and successor Henry IV, challenged enough by domestic threats to his rule, was not minded to renew hostilities.

CHAPTER 5

HENRY IV (1399-1413)

Henry IV

Henry usurped Richard II's throne. The problem of legitimacy, of Henry's right to the crown, was never resolved and it stimulated a succession of revolts. This was Henry's tragedy, for he desperately wanted to be accepted; and to establish a dynasty. In essence – in the absence of an unchallengeable dynastic claim – he ruled as king with the sanction of parliament, and so it remained.

But Henry, too, had advantages: he was a renowned soldier who had won distinction in campaigns abroad; he was the son of the great John of Gaunt (himself uncle of Richard II) and so heir – until

Richard appropriated them – to the massive estates pertaining to the dukes of Lancaster. He was father, too, of four militarily capable sons who, although still very young, could if needed take up the cudgels on his behalf; and they were, unlike the sons of his great predecessor Henry II, fundamentally loyal – if one excepts Prince Henry, frustrated and anxious to seize the sinews of power as his father's health declined. Above all perhaps, Henry was not Richard, who had proved increasingly arbitrary and wilful – to the extent of having his own uncle, the duke of Gloucester, accused of treason and murdered in the back room of a Calais inn.

Henry Bolingbroke (named after the Lincolnshire castle where he was born) landed at Ravenspur, Yorkshire in July 1399. Recently banished by Richard, he was returning to take possession of his inheritance, which was seized by Richard following Gaunt's death that January. That was all, 'to claim his own', or so (rather ambiguously) he said, and to insist on good government. Was he already aiming at the throne? Probably, but anyway events soon gathered an irresistible momentum of their own and Henry faced no significant opposition. King Richard himself was in Ireland.

Richard's support melted away. Soon he became a prisoner in the Tower where he signed a form of abdication. Next he was removed to Pontefract Castle where – following an early challenge to Henry's rule, the so-called 'Epiphany Rising' by Ricardian loyalists – he met his end; the official gloss that he starved himself to death was perhaps not widely believed. Be that as it may, if Henry could provide good government the likelihood was that he would find a wide measure of acceptance. The strong backing of his fellow exile Archbishop Thomas Arundel, whose elder brother, the earl of Arundel, had been executed for treason by Richard II, was crucial. This collaboration of king and archbishop would be a distinctive feature of the reign, and was quite unprecedented.

Following the suppression of the Epiphany Rising, Henry's first challenge came from an unexpected source: Wales. Here Owain Glyn Dŵr, the self-styled prince of Wales, fomented rebellion which, whilst not posing a direct challenge to Henry's government, proved a running sore for much of the reign and, besides, an encouragement to the king's enemies.

The Percy earls of Northumberland (along with their rivals, the Nevilles of Westmorland) were an essential bulwark against incursions from north of the border; they were vital no less in taming more general border lawlessness. As such they were indispensable, de facto monarchs in their own domain. Initially strong backers of Henry IV's challenge to Richard, they became his implacable adversaries. The Percy clan was headed by Earl Henry of Northumberland, sexagenarian and in character serpentine; the other key figures were his brother Thomas, earl of Worcester, Henry's appointee as Admiral of England and a Knight of the Garter – enjoying, therefore, the new king's absolute trust; and the scion of the dynasty, also Henry, the aptly named 'Hotspur', a renowned soldier and, too, a Knight of the Garter. (In reality Hotspur was himself three years older than Henry IV and a generation older than his son Prince Henry. For dramatic effect Shakespeare portrays Prince Henry and Hotspur as contemporaries and rivals.)

The betrayal of the Percys must have come as a fearful shock to Henry. Why did they break with him? The reasons suggested include: the king's refusal to ransom Hotspur's brother-in-law, Edmund Mortimer, uncle of the earl of March (a child with his own claim to the throne), who had been captured by Glyn Dŵr; his demand that the Percys give up the Scots prisoners they had captured in battle at Humbleton Hill; and his unwillingness to pay all the money owing them as wardens of the Scots Marches. It is also possible that they genuinely believed that Henry had simply returned to recover his inheritance. Perhaps, as 'kingmakers' before, they now underestimated Henry's strength.

In 1403 the Percys joined Glyn Dŵr and Mortimer (who had by now married Glyn Dŵr's daughter), in alleging Henry's 'perjury' and usurpation as their rebellion's justification. On hearing this news Henry gathered his forces and speedily marched westwards. The outcome of the battle of Shrewsbury (July 1403), in which the longbowmen proved especially lethal, was decided when Hotspur was killed. Certainly this was one of the bloodiest battles fought on English soil before Towton (1461). Hotspur's uncle, Worcester, was beheaded after the battle. His father, Northumberland, who was himself absent from the battlefield, subsequently disclaimed all knowledge of the plot. In the absence of any conclusive evidence to the contrary, it seemed politic to accept his protestations of innocence, and he was pardoned on condition that he surrendered his castles and offices; this decision may also be taken as reflecting Henry's own weakness. Still, the earl was clearly 'on probation' for his future good behaviour.

The next challenge (1405) to Henry had as its figurehead Richard Scrope, archbishop of York, himself with a Percy connection – and perhaps hoping that Northumberland's retainers also would participate. This rising was especially dangerous as it seemed to come with the Church's blessing. Scrope's list of grievances, posted on the gates of the city of York, brought several thousand out onto Shipton Moor. The manifesto highlighted the oppressive burden of taxation on the people, condemned the slaughter of nobles (no doubt with Hotspur and Worcester in mind) and the loss of territory in Wales; it also called for a meeting of parliament to remedy the grievances. The gathering on the moor was dissolved by guile. Scrope was arrested and beheaded. Henry's patience, so sorely tried, had finally snapped. Still, the precedent was an awkward one: no bishop, still less an archbishop, had been executed before. Archbishop Arundel, Scrope's fellow prelate, made a hasty, though in the event fruitless, ride north to try and dissuade Henry from his course. Pope Innocent VII issued a Bull excommunicating those responsible (though Arundel declined to publish it) but he soon died and the Bull was withdrawn.

The year 1405 may be seen as the turning point of the reign, at least in England. Internal rebellion had been brutally crushed; the threat posed by Glyn Dŵr (widely believed to be in collusion with the Percys – their scheming possibly involving a fantastic plan to partition England) had by then also subsided.

The only unfinished business remained the final showdown with Northumberland, now presumably feeling he had little to lose; the earl, having fled to Scotland, returned to fight and die at Bramham Moor (1408).

That Scrope's grievances were not without foundation is evident from an astonishingly frank letter addressed to the king by his confessor Philip Repingdon; remarkably, as early as 1401 it speaks of disappointed hopes: 'law and justice are banished from the realm…now our harp is tuned to mourning'. The note of disillusion is unmistakeable. Repingdon – subsequently bishop of Lincoln – is an interesting figure, enjoying a particular intimacy with the king: morally austere, probably with Lollard sympathies (certainly not a persecutor), he was a strong critic of clerical worldliness, uneasy about the Church's holding of temporalities, and was personally committed to the centrality of alms giving and the relief of poverty in Christian living. In his pastoral concerns Repingdon harked back to the example of his great predecessor in the see Bishop Robert Grosseteste – Matthew Paris says that Grosseteste, who may also have influenced Simon de Montfort's thinking, regarded himself as personally responsible for the spiritual wellbeing of every individual in the diocese; Lincoln was the largest diocese in England.

Around the time of Scrope's death Henry became seriously ill and disabling illnesses (a leg condition, skin disease, ulcers and probably circulation problems) afflicted him for his remaining years. There were, of course, those who attributed it to the execution of Scrope, whose tomb at York Minster attracted pilgrims in large numbers and where miracles were reported. Yet, for all the ravages of disease, Henry's will was indomitable. He was blessed too with a quartet of sons, Henry, Thomas, John and, of rather different character, his youngest Humphrey; the first three received great responsibility at a very early age, and it is notable how well they acquitted themselves of their father's trust. His eldest Henry, prince of Wales, understandably frustrated and with an eye to the future, became a focus for those who despaired of the king's inability to solve his problems; Henry Beaufort, bishop of Winchester, the prince's half-uncle and former tutor, a man of great wealth and considerable ability, was a close confidant in his designs. The ailing king and charismatic prince fell out seriously in 1412 over policy towards France, always Henry's foremost foreign concern. Henry IV desired a lasting peace with France or at least to maintain the truce for as long as possible; the retention of Guyenne and Calais he regarded as paramount.

Beyond Henry's immediate family, his friend Archbishop Arundel was an immense source of strength. Arundel saw service as chancellor of the realm, was a frequent attender at the council and was present at all the parliaments. He was instrumental in securing from the Canterbury convocation the subsidies which Henry urgently needed; and he lent the king lavish sums of money (only Bishop Beaufort lent more). Arundel must take much of the credit for working to restore solvency to crown finance. Henry was careful to make requests to parliament only when all other financial resources had been exhausted. Sources of royal income included crown lands, income from justice and from the system of customs and duties; enjoying the wide revenues of the duchy of Lancaster was a boon. Henry never tried to intimidate the Commons and, as a result, despite the inevitable complaints of unnecessary extravagance and unworthy courtiers, their relationship was not especially fraught.

Church and state acted in concert to eradicate heresy. Arundel was relentlessly severe in his persecution of heretics; his fierce opposition to Lollardy associated the crown with religious orthodoxy. In 1401 a statute 'For the Burning of a Heretic', supported by the king, Arundel and majority opinion in the Commons, prescribed the burning of relapsed heretics and followed on that of William Sawtre, a tailor from Evesham. According to the statute the bishops were empowered to hand over to the secular authorities those who had relapsed or refused to abjure; the condemned were to be burnt 'in a high place'. Until 1410, however, no further Lollards were executed.

Henry genuinely believed – perhaps with Edward III as an exemplar – in a consensual approach to politics. In part this reflected his own insecurity, for he could never shake off the taint of usurpation. In more auspicious circumstances, and without disabling health conditions, he might have proved a highly effective ruler. With his sons at his side one may almost speak of a Lancastrian family government. Princes Henry and Thomas had serious disagreements, and Prince Henry's later relationship with his father was at times deeply unsettled – he was marginalised in 1412 during the ailing king's rapprochement with Thomas over their anti-Burgundian policy. Nevertheless, rivalries and policy disagreements were contained (unlike in France). In the midst of life's tribulations the king assuredly will have found consolation in the strength of his family ties. Henry's relationships with both his wives, Mary de Bohun (the mother of his sons) and Joan of Navarre, appear to have been amicable and affectionate, and with Joan he shared an interest in music. Henry remembered and also made provision for his household servants in his will.

'Uneasy lies the head that wears a crown': of no other English monarch can this more truly be said. As he lay dying and in great pain, Henry must have had many sins on his conscience, which only God might forgive. He will have been painfully aware of his failure to live up to the high ideals of Philip Repingdon. In his will, that of a 'sinful wretch', he craves God's mercy for a misspent life and his people's pardon. His achievement – in the circumstances of the reign no mean feat – was to have survived.

CHAPTER 6

HENRY V (1413-1422)

Henry V

Henry V is England's iconic warrior king, the victor of Agincourt. A master of organisation and planning, this Henry is by common consent regarded as one of the ablest men to have sat on the English throne. In character he was brutally single-minded and possessed of a certain charisma that many found irresistible. His legacy though, a baby son as his heir and his renewal of the French war, was to prove toxic.

* * *

If Shakespeare's *Henry V* is not to be numbered among his most compelling dramas, the problem may lie with its subject. Ambiguity, character and motivation: such are the issues that fascinate the dramatist. About the man Henry there may seem little that is ambiguous. Yet the language resonates still, down the centuries. In times of war, if some have found consolation in Anthony Trollope's arcadian vision of Barsetshire, more surely will have been fortified by *Henry V*. 'O, for a Muse of fire!' – sorely needed in a diminished England, post-Brexit. 'Now all the youth of England are on fire!' Such lines come to mind now, incomparably delivered by that great Welsh actor Emrys James ('Chorus' to Alan Howard's 'Henry') at Stratford all of 50 years ago. 'Harry, England and St George!', 'Once more unto the breach, dear friends!' A rich seam surely to be mined by football coaches in the dressing room. And why neglected? 'Ignorance, pure ignorance' (to quote Dr Johnson), one must presume.

*   *   *

Henry's relationship with his father, especially during the latter's declining years, had been uneasy, indeed crisis-ridden. Prior to that, at the battle of Shrewsbury (1403) the prince had distinguished himself by sustaining a serious injury by an arrow wound in the face but refusing to leave the field. Probably he owed his life to the battlefield ministrations of the ingenious royal surgeon John Bradmore who extracted the arrowhead buried in his face, and left an account of the procedure he adopted. (This injury may well account for the familiar side profile depiction of Henry's face.)

Whilst some of the detail of Shakespeare's account of Prince Henry's riotous youth may invite scepticism, he still has that knack of seeing to the heart of the matter. Certainly the prince was impatient to take control. According to the contemporary chronicler Thomas Walsingham, and slightly later sources also, there was truly a very remarkable change in Henry following his accession, and this may of itself give credence to the familiar picture of a dissolute youth. The new king was a 'new man': a serious-minded and unimpeachably orthodox son of the Church. Both the Bridgettine and the austere Carthusian orders benefitted from the king's patronage. Henry's confessors, constantly at hand, were drawn from the order of Carmelite friars. Gravitas and a deep sense of personal responsibility became his hallmarks; such behaviour alone befitted an anointed king commissioned by God. His interests in theological reading and religious devotion now became conspicuous. Within months of Henry's accession Richard II received an honourable reburial in Westminster Abbey, so contributing to the spread of reconciliation (though it failed to scotch all rumours that Richard was still alive).

At this time there were indications that the basis of Catholic faith, handed down over the generations, was beginning to be questioned. The new ideas were associated with the brilliant and controversial Oxford theologian John Wyclif (died 1384). Wyclif – once employed as a diplomat in the royal service – had enjoyed the protective patronage of John of Gaunt, Henry's grandfather. He believed in the Bible in English, doubted transubstantiation (the miracle of the Mass), and challenged the Church's historic teaching on the sacraments; he argued that bishops should not be employed in politics (this was corrupting); and that the Scriptures were the only valid foundation for any authority. Instead of the Church's authority, people should turn to the Bible as the only basis of divine truth. Wyclif also rediscovered the writings of Bishop Robert Grosseteste, who in the mid-13th century had lambasted the state of the Church for worldliness, not sparing the pope and cardinals. One of Wyclif's notions was especially revolutionary – and potentially explosive! He taught that authority could only be exercised legitimately by a person in a state of grace. But how could it be objectively determined who was in such an enviable state? Were bishops and clergy, even monarchs? This notion had the potential to subvert all authority both in Church and state. Wyclif's ideas began to be diffused more widely. People, often artisans and even women, met to discuss them, even at considerable personal risk. Those who accepted Wyclif's critique were dismissively known as 'Lollards' (the word signifies mumblers who spoke nonsense).

The first burning for heresy, that of William Sawtre, was in London in 1401. Prince Henry was himself present at the burning of John Badby, a tailor, in 1410 for his denial of transubstantiation and seems to have remonstrated with the unfortunate man – he ordered the fire to be extinguished while Badby was urged to recant – but to no avail. Be that as it may, to modern readers the scene feels utterly grotesque. Henry was certainly orthodox – of that there can be no doubt!

'Political Lollardy' became a threat in the rebellion of Sir John Oldcastle (January 1414), a former confidant of Henry's and a man of some consequence in his native Herefordshire. One may believe that Oldcastle was persuaded by wandering Lollard preachers, more certainly by reading Lollard texts. Oldcastle's design was to capture the king and his brothers during the Christmas celebrations while a nationally raised force of Lollards was to seize the city of London. The impression is sometimes given of a rather madcap venture but at the time the threat seemed real enough. Henry, forewarned of the plan, acted, as always, decisively; he closed the city gates and smashed the heretical knight's rebellion. Forty-five persons were executed (principally hanged as traitors rather than burnt for heresy). Oldcastle himself remained at large until late 1417 when he was apprehended, condemned, hanged and burnt. To the end he maintained his hostility to authority and to the Church; and – as a parting shot – he prophesised that he would rise on the third day. Anyway, by then Lollardy, tainted with treason and subversion, was finished as a political force.

During his brief reign Henry spent more than half his time in France. In his absence a trustworthy lieutenant – one or other of his three brothers – was empowered to act for him, his actions being subject to 'the approval of the council' (comprising nine persons), though Henry, characteristically, reserved to himself all key decisions. Much reliance was placed upon his uncle, the chancellor Henry Beaufort, bishop of Winchester and his successor Thomas Langley, bishop of Durham. With parliament (which met every year except 1418 and 1422) Henry, despite his absence abroad, had a generally amicable relationship based on mutual understanding.

Before the embarkation from Southampton for France – and the preparation was characteristically meticulous – Henry had to confront a quite different conspiracy against his person, and from an unexpected source. Whilst the precise motivation of the men involved in the Southampton Plot – Sir Thomas Grey, Henry's own cousin Richard, earl of Cambridge, and Henry, Lord Scrope – remains somewhat obscure, their purpose was clear enough: the king's assassination. The involvement of Scrope, formerly treasurer of England (and nephew of Richard Scrope, the archbishop of York, who was executed by Henry IV in 1405), was viewed by contemporaries as especially shocking. The plot betrayed, the sentences of death were speedily carried out. Henry again acted decisively, showing no indulgence. Such resolution (as with the Oldcastle affair) can only have enhanced his reputation. Within a week, on 11 August 1415, the fleet set sail for France to recover what Henry saw as his 'just rights'. He demanded both the French throne and the English possessions as laid down at the Treaty of Brétigny (1360), which had given Edward III control over all south-west France; most of the gains of Brétigny had since been recovered by France. But all this was to beg the crucial, and unanswered, question: Were these perceived as Henry's personal (or his dynasty's) 'rights', or those of his nation?

The intermittently-waged Hundred Years War between England and France had been in abeyance since Richard II's closing years. The French, though themselves deeply divided, seem to have had a poor opinion of Henry as a military leader; the dauphin's (the French crown prince) sending of a gift of tennis balls to Henry (quite possibly true), recounted to memorable effect by Shakespeare, is indicative of their valuation.

From Henry's point of view, for a domestic audience, the renewal of the war with the historic enemy would buy national unity and, if successful, silence any residual doubts about the dynasty's legitimacy (always his father's Achilles heel). For nobles there was the prospect of glory, grants of land, plunder and cash for ransoms of prisoners taken. That said, the risks were very great. Whatever the outcome, lives (both English and French) would be destroyed and large tracts of land devastated. One may wonder if such thoughts entered Henry's mind. It may be doubted. After all this was God's cause, prosecuted by His human viceroy and He would vouchsafe victory. The sieges of Rouen and Meaux, in particular, would in time visit appalling suffering upon the civilian population. At Rouen Henry had gibbets constructed in view of the wall on which he hanged prisoners. Rouen was the largest city to be taken by siege (January 1419) during the Hundred Years War; it lasted six months.

Henry was undeniably an outstanding military commander. At Agincourt, for instance, one may cite his decision to place six-foot-long stakes in the ground to protect his archers against the expected French cavalry attack; the effective deployment of his archers; his astute positioning; the strict discipline he imposed on his troops and the hard line he took with camp followers; and his own personal valour.

The war was prosecuted successfully from Henry's standpoint. The Treaty of Troyes (May 1420) was the high watermark of English power in France: a French king formally recognised the claim of English kings to the French crown. Henry now styled himself 'heir and regent of France'. On 2 June 1420 Henry and Catherine of Valois, daughter of the French king, Charles VI, were married 'for the benefit of peace'. Nonetheless, the treaty raised anxieties in parliament: concerns about the subordination of the English to the French part of the 'dual polity' were expressed. Henry was himself absent from the British Isles for three full years between 1418 and 1421. The opinion was strongly expressed that the French territories should bear the cost of their defence and administration.

In December 1421 Henry's queen, Catherine, gave birth to a son. By November, however, Henry's health was giving rise to serious concern. Still he transacted business with his customary energy and foresight. When he died, aged only 35, in August 1422 his passing was (it is reported) lamented in France no less than in England. His sagacity and firmness was an instructive contrast to French internal anarchy and the problems caused by the mental disability of Charles VI. Henry V was an outstandingly able and charismatic leader, but it was, above all, French political disunity and Burgundy's feud with France (the duke of Burgundy became Henry's firm ally), that proved his greatest advantage.

Whilst assuming the moral high ground is no business of the historian, the ultimate question cannot be ducked: Why, for more than 100 years, albeit with interludes, were two Christian nations in arms against each other – and finally to no conceivable purpose? John Wyclif had been one voice that considered warfare between Christian nations as being contrary to God's commandment to love one's neighbour. In the following century the much maligned Cardinal Wolsey praised peace as a good and holy thing; both Thomas More and the brilliant Christian humanist scholar Erasmus believed in universal comity between Christian nations. It seems that at the end of his life Henry claimed that he had invaded France simply because his cause was just and he desired to bring lasting peace. However, if Henry had any plans for the organisation of a united Anglo-French state they died with him. As has justly been said, the worst disaster of his reign was his premature death.

CHAPTER 7

HENRY VI (1422-1461 & 1470-1471)

Henry VI

Henry VI is the most tragic of English kings. Just nine months old when his all-conquering father died, he lived long enough to see the ruin of the English position in France and the onset of the Wars of the Roses, of which he was a hapless spectator. Finally, his own life was taken.

Henry was a man of exemplary piety, more a saint than a king, according to his former chaplain John Blacman's account, written after the king's death: he was more given to prayer 'than practising vain sports and pursuits'. In the course of his life Henry was also afflicted by serious mental disability. There were times when he was unable to participate in affairs at all, still less in his country's governance. Inevitably this vacuum at the centre created huge problems, for it ran counter to all expectations of medieval kingship. Whether or not Henry was actively and personally involved in decision-making remains to this day a controversial area. Certainly he seems to have been far more focused on the next world than present earthly realities.

In character Henry V and his son were utterly dissimilar, their piety apart: the one supremely confident in his own ability, and possessing a clear conception of the main tasks of kingship; the other more suited for a life of prayer, perhaps under the guidance of a benevolent abbot.

*   *   *

Henry V's premature death caused widespread shock – in France no less than in England. The prospect of a lengthy royal minority, with all its uncertainties, was hardly one to relish. The overriding concern of the regency council that assumed power was to buttress the English position in France. Of the child-king's surviving uncles – Thomas, duke of Clarence (probably Henry IV's favourite son) had been killed in France in 1421 – John, duke of Bedford, who became regent of France, was a man of great ability, both in the military and political spheres, and enjoyed widespread respect; Humphrey, duke of Gloucester (the 'good duke' of myth) was more self-seeking and less consensual. Both men were noted collectors of books and patrons of men of letters. Bedford too had in his service the great musician John Dunstable. The other key figure was Cardinal Henry Beaufort, bishop of Winchester, the child's great-uncle, a skilled politician who repeatedly loaned huge sums to the royal government.

Despite serious personal differences the council in many ways played its challenging hand with considerable credit. Bedford's steadiness and his ability to exercise some check upon rivalries was crucial. That said, it was probably inevitable that sooner or later effective French leadership would emerge – as it did under Charles VII – with the avowed aim of expelling the English, whose cause suffered a major setback anyway with Bedford's death in 1435. The same year saw another blow: the defection of England's principal ally, the duke of Burgundy, who was reconciled with the French king.

The child-king's English coronation was in 1429. His French, in accordance with the Treaty of Troyes (1420), which recognised Henry as heir to the throne of France, followed at the end of 1431 when he was aged 10. His earliest formation was entrusted to his governess Lady Alice Butler, who was empowered to administer (as the English say) 'reasonable chastisement'; and later to the respected earl of Warwick with a brief, doubtless, to induct the boy into the manly virtues. No doubt his mother Queen Catherine would have had regular contact. By 1436 decisions were headed, 'the King with the advice of council'. The council's formal tutelage was now at an end.

The English position in France was by this time facing serious challenges. The priorities had to be the defence of Normandy, Gascony in the south-west and above all – for both military and commercial reasons – Calais, with which the duke of Gloucester was entrusted. Gloucester was vehemently opposed to making any concessions to the French. France, however, was most unlikely to accept the permanent loss of Normandy, any more than the English would abandon Henry's claim to the French throne. In the opposite camp to Gloucester were Cardinal Beaufort and William de la Pole, duke of Suffolk, the rising man at court, who advocated a peace policy – in accord, one must assume, with the young king's own wishes (the shedding of Christian blood was always anathema to Henry). Certainly the duke of Bedford's statesmanlike ability to maintain a semblance of unity between the factions, even when in France as he usually was, was sorely missed.

Henry, who abhorred nakedness, lest he be 'snared by unlawful desires', was described as 'more religious than a man of religion'. This compulsive religiosity became perhaps obsessive. Henry's piety most truly found its focus in the royal foundations of Eton College (1440) and King's College, Cambridge (1441); King's Chapel was only finally completed in Henry VIII's time. These were the only really positive achievements of Henry's reign. He laid the foundation stones of both, took an intensely personal interest and committed massive financial resources, which might (it was asserted) have been better employed in the defence of the English position in France. There were complaints about this expenditure in parliament and royal profligacy more generally was sharply criticised. Henry's patronage of learning and the universities was likewise a statement about his devotional life.

Henry's deep piety might be – and was – applauded but medieval kingship demanded infinitely more. Henry crucially neglected the principal and personal duty of any medieval king: the defence and advancement of his own and his kingdom's rights and interests. That he showed no interest in leading an army to France ran counter to all expectations of the time and was in itself deeply problematic.

Henry's governance of England was severely flawed. The king's generosity – basically he found it impossible to say 'no' to the myriad of petitioners seeking favours – was a crucial failing. Existing ownership was not checked as a matter of course; indeed, the same land might be granted to two different men (even on consecutive days). The operation of justice was deeply impaired by the issuing of royal pardons. Men found guilty even of murder might be pardoned on account of an approaching religious feast in the Church's calendar. The alienation of crown lands and offices much reduced the crown's income.

Henry's personal decision to release – and without ransom! – the duke of Orléans, captured at Agincourt in 1415, was deeply controversial and unpopular. It also completely failed to lead to Henry's greatly desired peace.

Attempts to defend Normandy after 1435 were made: first by Richard, duke of York, who was sent with a significant force, and then (disastrously) by the duke of Somerset. Next Henry sent new envoys, including the duke of Suffolk, to France. It was agreed that Henry would marry Margaret, daughter of René, duke of Anjou (an important French nobleman); additionally, in a deeply unpopular concession, Henry personally decided to hand over all English lands in Maine to René in return for a 20-year truce between England and France. But now the French king, Charles VII, seized Normandy and Gascony was also lost. Finally, the Hundred Years War ended with the disastrous English defeat at Castillon (July 1453). In all of this Henry had failed to provide any personal military leadership.

* * *

In May 1450 Cade's Rebellion broke out in Kent and the insurgents were joined by men from Sussex. Significantly, the rebels pinned their hopes on Duke Richard of York as the man who would restore good order and governance. The widely hated duke of Suffolk, Henry's leading minister, had already been beheaded by pirates on board ship when leaving for exile; other officials, including senior clerics with court connections such as bishops Moleyns and Aiscough, were butchered. As always, the counsellors, not the king himself, were held responsible for the calamitous state of affairs. Those who killed Suffolk – held responsible for the deeply unpopular cession of Maine to the French – and the rest saw themselves as loyal subjects, doing dirty work on their king's behalf. What these events also showed was a lack of consistency in Henry's approach. When the rebellion was put down, Henry first opted for clemency and then abandoned it for brutal suppression, hence what became known as 'the harvest of heads'.

Margaret of Anjou, aged 15 when she married Henry (himself 23) in 1445, proved to be of quite different mettle from her spouse: active, assertive, full-blooded. Naturally enough, she desired peace with France and became closely identified with Suffolk's (and Cardinal Beaufort's) policy to this end. Gloucester, still maintaining his opposition, was tarnished by association when his wife Eleanor Cobham was convicted of compassing the king's death by sorcery. Placed under arrest at a meeting of parliament, Gloucester died in 1447 (the circumstances are unclear) while awaiting trial. Within a few weeks his long-term rival and antagonist Beaufort, the most experienced politician in the country, followed him to the grave. Queen Margaret brought a new and challenging dimension to politics. A sort of hybrid of Boudica and Mrs Thatcher, she was utterly uncompromising in her commitment to her husband and later her son and to the Lancastrian cause. As a dominating woman in the male world of politics and warfare, she was bound to attract deep hostility.

Duke Richard of York became the principal antagonist of the Lancastrians after the Cade Rebellion. As a former loyal lieutenant of France and then of Ireland, he had shown proven leadership capability. York was the king's kinsman and in his own right possessed a perfectly reasonable claim to the throne (back to Edward III's son Lionel). Queen Margaret was always fiercely antagonistic towards York who, as the crisis deepened, aimed for the crown himself.

In August 1453 Henry suffered a total mental and physical collapse, quite possibly caused by the final defeat in France and mounting domestic turmoil. He fell into a state of inertia lasting 18 months. Not even the birth of a long-awaited son, Edward, could evince a reaction from him – there were even those who voiced doubts about the child's paternity. Such a breakdown was quite unprecedented in an English adult king. The partial and unpredictable recoveries that Henry experienced only made the situation worse, leading to renewed factionalism and instability. The political elite must have been left in a huge quandary.

In these circumstances York was realistically – in the view of most nobles and probably commoners too – the only person to turn to, and he was duly appointed (after some delay) Protector of England in March 1454. Henry's partial recovery at the end of the year, ending York's protectorate, in a way only made things worse. York's bitter rival Somerset, blamed for the loss of Normandy, returned as the leading minister. Moves were made against York, who had the backing of his allies, the earl of Salisbury and his son, the earl of Warwick (later known as 'the Kingmaker'). There followed a military showdown at St Albans (May 1455), often regarded as the start of the Wars of the Roses. In a notable dereliction of duty, Henry, remaining a passive spectator, declined to engage in any negotiations with the protagonists. In the battle Somerset was killed and Henry was himself wounded in the neck by an arrow. The victorious Yorkists now had possession of the king.

York, reappointed Protector of the Realm, now sought to implement his programme of reform: the restoration of law and order and the crown's finances, and punishment for those who had misled the king. Unsurprisingly, he failed to attract sufficient support for the passing of an Act of Resumption, aimed at annulling many of Henry's grants of land and office; too many vested interests were affected. The ending of York's protectorate (February 1456) also marked the end of the last attempt to provide effective government in Henry VI's reign. A period of turmoil then led to civil war.

Henry's weakness and fragile health was at the root of the tumult. Still, the striking fact is that until well after the outbreak of hostilities his legitimacy as king was very generally accepted. The fight was rather over who should have control of him.

Queen Margaret was acknowledged, by friend and foe alike, to be the figurehead of the Lancastrian cause. But her abrasive personality, and doubtless her gender also, raised many hackles. She was fiercely determined that her young son would succeed his father. Henry, by contrast, when captured by the Yorkists at the battle of Northampton in July 1460, apparently meekly acquiesced in a compromise whereby his own son would be disinherited in favour of York as heir to the throne. In March 1458 there was a staged event aimed at bringing the two sides together, the so-called 'Loveday', when the two factions walked in procession through London to St Paul's Church. Royal policy, though, was deeply inconsistent. It varied from apparent attempted reconciliation with the Yorkists to outright hostility. There can be little doubt though that Margaret, fiery and tempestuous, had a visceral loathing of the Yorkists. This was always going to be a massive obstacle to any settlement. York, if one sets his undoubted personal ambition aside, was understandably frustrated at Henry's inability to provide good governance. The Yorkists too – accused of treason as a great council held at Coventry in June 1459 – had entirely reasonable concerns about their own safety.

In late 1460 York, for the first time, claimed the throne in parliament in place of Henry. This claim met with much resistance;

the displacement of the hereditary principle was seen by many as subversive of the natural order of things. Instead parliament passed an Act of Accord, whereby York was granted the protectorate during Henry's lifetime and, after the king's death, the succession. Henry's son, Prince Edward, was disinherited. Shortly afterwards York was himself killed at the battle of Wakefield (December 1460). His ally Salisbury was beheaded (or lynched), York's head adorned with a paper crown. The Yorkist baton was now passed on to his 18-year-old son Edward, earl of March. Edward, having been crowned Edward IV, went on to overwhelm the Lancastrian forces at the battle of Towton (March 1461), fought in a snowstorm – on Palm Sunday! Whilst the number of casualties must be conjectural, this was probably the bloodiest battle yet fought on English soil. One thing is certain: Henry would have been profoundly shaken by the shedding of so much Christian blood.

It is almost impossible to conceive the level of bitterness engendered by the civil war and the atrocities that became, almost as a matter of course, accepted. After each battle came the settling of scores: for the vanquished lords, who had not made good their flight, retribution typically came at the hands of the executioner. It feels a world apart from the almost civilised decorum of the age of chivalry!

Henry, his wife and son, who had not been present at Towton, now found safety across the Scottish border. In 1463 Margaret and her son, Edward, sailed for France, where they set up a court in exile in her father's domains. Eventually deprived of Scottish support, Henry's fugitive existence ended with his capture (June 1465) in a forest known as Clitherwood. For the following five years Henry was a prisoner, apparently well-enough treated, in the Tower.

The final twist came with Henry's Readeption (meaning 'reattainment of royal power'), caused by Yorkist divisions, for a few months from October 1470. Edward IV was himself forced to flee the realm and Warwick 'the Kingmaker' engineered Henry's return to the throne. Then Edward returned from exile with an army, entered London and took custody of Henry. He defeated Warwick at the battle of Barnet (April 1471), where 'the Kingmaker' was slain. Edward finally overcame the forces of Queen Margaret and Prince Edward at the 'bloody meadow' of Tewkesbury (4 May). Margaret was captured and her son was killed trying to flee the field. All that remained was for Henry to be deprived of his life, presumably on Edward's direct order, on 21 May. (The Yorkist spin that he died of 'displeasure and melancholy' may be viewed with justified scepticism.)

Henry's widow, Margaret, packed off back to France, spent her remaining years on her father's estates, subsisting on a meagre pension from the French king. For her husband, her son and the Lancastrian cause she had given – for better or worse – her all, and she paid the ultimate price: the loss of everything she held dear. She had lived to witness the triumph of her dynasty's enemies, not in the person of Duke Richard himself, but in that of his son. This triumph, though, would in time itself prove hollow. If only her husband had possessed even a modest share of her own spirit! How, one is tempted to reflect, she must have rued the day when she first sighted the 'sceptr'd isle'! In a later age Queen Catherine of Aragon – though for quite different reasons – might well have similar thoughts.

*　　*　　*

The root of Henry's problems lay in his unwillingness, or inability, to engage in the governance of his realm in any consistent or sustained way; and, crucially, in his total failure to provide leadership, especially military leadership. The abbot of St Albans called him 'half-witted in affairs of state'. A passive figure, he seems to have been malleable to the wishes of whoever had control of him at any particular time. A preoccupation with 'higher things' was simply not an option for any medieval monarch. It was in fact a dereliction of duty. Henry's mental illness, probably a hereditary condition, was itself a human tragedy. The massive vacuum at the centre was filled by Queen Margaret and also, from time to time, by the duke of York: bitter rivals, both were deeply controversial and divisive figures. In the end the matter was settled by force – and York's son Edward IV acted decisively.

During a deeply troubled life Henry VI gave much thought to death. It is known that he spent time at Westminster Abbey planning the location of his tomb. His desire was to be buried next to Henry III, another pious king afflicted by civil strife. According to the chronicle of the prior of Crowland Abbey, he most urgently prayed 'that he might be admitted into the brotherhood of our monastery'. Alas, the accident of birth did not allow for this. Henry's buildings, the foundations at Eton and Cambridge, are his legacy to the world. Finally, though, the man who commissioned them remains an enigma.

CHAPTER 8

HENRY VII (1485-1509)

Henry VII

Henry VII is the accountant manqué, the supreme businessman among the kings of England. He accrued money, checked the books and, in the fullness of time, garnered international respect. He established a large measure of domestic peace and order. If his achievements were by no means spectacular – certainly not of the sort to fire the imagination of dramatists – they laid the foundations for the Tudor dynasty's future. To this day, however, the reign, especially in the latter stages, remains controversial, even hard fought over.

Part of the problem in assessing this Henry's character may be felt to lie in the absence of contemporary chroniclers (such as those that enliven the accounts of the reigns of the first two Henrys) to provide colour and 'inside information'; hence the characteristically 'enigmatic' feel of the man.

With hindsight we know that the Wars of the Roses finally burnt themselves out with the death of Richard III at the battle of Bosworth (August 1485). But hindsight is a dangerous thing, especially in the historian. In 1485 few men would have placed bets on Henry Tudor's survival. But survive he did and, in course of time, he prospered.

The Yorkist dynasty, following the demise of Henry VI, showed a fatal tendency to self-destruct. A basically capable king, Edward IV, the eldest son of Richard duke of York, ruled (with one brief interlude – the Readeption of Henry VI) from 1461 to 1483. He put an end to civil conflict, brought a degree of political stability and order, and provided some years of respite from overseas war and trade conflict. He did much to restore the prestige of the monarchy. Of his younger brothers, George, duke of Clarence, was put to death (traditionally by drowning in a butt of malmsey wine) in the Tower on grounds of treason; Richard, who was loyal, survived. Edward's premature and unexpected death threw the Yorkist interest into disarray. Richard came out on top, ruthlessly disposing of his enemies in the process, including (in all probability) his nephews, Edward's sons, the princes in the Tower. Richard III ruled, in the face of considerable disquiet and not insignificant opposition, from 1483 to 1485. Henry Tudor prevailed at Bosworth, but it could have gone either way. Many men, after decades of blood-letting, were not minded to commit themselves.

* * *

Henry's first 14 years (he was born in 1457) were spent in Wales, and his grandfather Owen Tudor was wholly Welsh. Certainly he owed a great deal on the way to Bosworth to Welsh support, or at least abstention from active opposition. However, Henry's claim to the crown, which came through the Lancastrian line, was scarcely compelling: his mother Margaret – a notably able woman, renowned for her piety – was the last of the Beauforts, John of Gaunt's descendants. Still, this lineage – there was no royal ancestry on the male side – was sufficient to attract to Henry, in growing numbers, men desirous of Richard's overthrow; some of these were persuaded to join him in the life of exile in Brittany. For Henry, though, victory at Bosworth was vindication enough; it stamped him with God's approval.

Others, however, might see things differently: the daughters of Edward IV, for example, and Clarence's son, the earl of Warwick (a boy of 10) were personages to be taken into account. Henry married Elizabeth, the eldest of these daughters, and placed the boy in the Tower. Rumours, though, continued to abound: some said the princes in the Tower lived still, others that the boy Warwick was at large again. Lambert Simnel (also aged 10) was engaged by Richard Simons, a priest, to impersonate Warwick; he was proclaimed Edward VI at Dublin. The Yorkists had been popular in Ireland. Ireland in fact was always problematic, and not just for the Tudors; faction-fighting was rife among Anglo-Irish lords of dubious loyalty, and Ireland was always a potential springboard for invasion. Battle was joined in June 1487 at Stoke, where both Simnel and Simons fell into Henry's hands. Simnel began a career as a scullion in the royal kitchens – a comment perhaps on Henry's rather sardonic humour – and subsequently rose to be king's falconer; Simons was imprisoned for life.

Four years later another Yorkist pretender, Perkin Warbeck, manifested himself to the world, this time as Richard, the younger prince in the Tower, from where he had somehow escaped. Henry seems to have treated this 'Richard', who remained a dangerous menace, with an almost bemused indulgence even following his arrest and full confession. However, the king's leniency was abused. Warbeck was tried on a charge of trying to escape from the Tower and in November 1499 was hanged. At the same time – all this is rather mysterious – the hapless earl of Warwick was brought from the Tower, convicted of treason (which he admitted) and beheaded. Still, it must be admitted that in dealing with these challenges Henry had shown a degree of forbearance, characteristic of his nature, and even a wry humour, which was altogether wanting in his second son and eventual successor.

Meanwhile there were more plots at home, now involving the Stanleys, the family which had really put Henry on the throne; and threats too from the de la Pole family. These and others were resolutely dealt with.

The hard experience of life, the exile years especially, had taught Henry Tudor to be cautious; he was never a man for rash or vainglorious undertakings. A solitary child, he never really gave himself away in later life. Vesting confidence in a man was not a thing to be undertaken lightly. Henry was certainly shrewd in his choice of ministers and servants (often churchmen), many of whom repaid his trust with a lifetime of loyal service: Cardinal Morton, Bishop Fox, William Warham, Reginald Bray, Thomas Lovell, Richard Empson and Edmund Dudley (the last two to become the first fruits of his son's murderous fury) were amongst them. In place of the great nobles, Henry's counsellors were drawn from men of lower rank ('new men'), who were wholly dependent upon him. Their authority was based on their membership of the royal council. Faction was largely absent from his reign; unlike his successor, he set himself apart and was not a man easily manipulated.

Parliament functioned only intermittently. Only seven parliaments – important principally for tax-raising purposes – were summoned during the reign; between 1485 and 1497 there were 10 sessions, with an average duration of six weeks, but the remainder of the reign saw only one parliament (1504). In peacetime there was an expectation that kings would be self-sufficient and 'live of their own'. The tradition had grown up that taxation should be raised only with the consent of parliament.

In Henry's reign the Court of Star Chamber (meeting under a star-spangled ceiling at the Palace of Westminster), comprising the king's counsellors and judges, became a busy and increasingly popular supplement to the regular justice of the common law courts; it enforced the law when other courts were unable to do so because of corruption and influence. In the following reign the judicial activity of Star Chamber grew rapidly; Thomas Wolsey, as chancellor, encouraged suitors to appeal to it in the first instance, rather than after they had failed to find remedy in the ordinary courts.

The crown lands and customs were the most significant elements in Henry's ordinary revenue. Following the end of the Wars of the Roses Henry inherited large tracts of land. The attainders of the reign – acts of parliament declaring a person guilty of a serious crime, often treason, and their lands forfeited – brought in more. Where his predecessors had sold crown lands for cash, or granted them away, Henry collected land; this was the most solid basis for the royal finances. Resumption replaced alienation. Collecting customs revenue, which Henry urgently desired to increase, was more problematic; collection at the ports was difficult and smuggling flourished.

In foreign trade Henry's chief activity was to encourage the export of cloth; he attempted to promote and protect the industry at home. He sought to promote trade agreements with foreign powers, especially with Archduke Philip, ruler of England's most important market, the Low Countries.

Henry's marriage to Elizabeth of York, who died in 1503, appears to have been happy enough, though of eight children born, five predeceased him. His grief at her passing will only have been exceeded by the early death in April 1502 of his son Arthur (the choice of name itself significant – and with hindsight, one might think, tempting providence), the hope of the dynasty. Arthur's short-lived marriage to the Spanish princess, Catherine of Aragon, is itself testimony to the rise of England in European estimation; and this was Henry's doing. His alliance with Spain arose from common and long-standing hostility to France. Ever present in the background, we may not doubt, was Margaret Beaufort, the formidable matriarch of the family, ever solicitous for her son's and the dynasty's future.

In religion Henry was conventionally orthodox and pious. He kept a firm control over episcopal appointments and remained on cordial terms with the papacy. The tradition of close alliance between the bishops and the crown was firmly established. About 70 persons are known to have been tried for heresy during the reign, nearly all of whom abjured.

At the same time Henry VII has never been short of detractors, even from the earliest times, his 'avarice' being singled out for particular censure. Polydore Vergil, an Italian chronicler resident in England, observed that from about 1502 Henry 'began to treat his people with more harshness and severity than had been his custom in order (as the king himself asserted) to ensure that they remained more thoroughly and entirely in obedience to him'.

From the outset Henry aimed to squeeze all that was possible out of his feudal rights, and his exactions – albeit within the law – came to be resented by many of his leading subjects. His high-handed methods, use of attainders and his treatment of the nobility have been evinced as indicators of 'tyranny'. The system of bonds and recognizances, especially after 1502, was greatly extended and widely resented. Those fined for offences committed, or forced to enter bonds for their future good behaviour, were bound to pay huge amounts of money. In this way a chain of obligation was created. Over the reign as a whole perhaps only a quarter of the peerage families remained free of these financial penalties, either on their own behalf or as sureties for others.

Was Henry motivated purely by avarice? At the close of his reign there was a balance in the order of £1.5 million, a veritable treasure chest for his successor. Undoubtedly, though, there was huge resentment – as his servant Edmund Dudley, when under sentence of death in the Tower, later acknowledged. Dudley in his confession referred to 84 cases of unjust exactions for which he believed the execution of Henry VII's will should make remedy. People had paid huge fines or been imprisoned for 'light matters' based on 'light surmise'. Dudley pressed for his royal master's will to be carried out in the matter of reparation. In his will Henry did reveal an awareness that he might have gone too far in his exactions. Still the whole system, however abhorrent, was surely more humane than his son's more savage alternatives.

And there is another side to Henry: a more attractive figure than the caricature of the dour, aloof, scrooge-like figure, immersed in checking the books, bent over his counting table and devoted to the practice of avarice. He rewarded Welsh bards and kept St David's Day. When on progress, it is reported that he kept a company of his numerous minstrels, trumpeters, harpists and pipers; he distributed largesse to all kinds of people who brought him presents. Let it not be forgotten either that he treated Lambert Simnel and, initially, Perkin Warbeck with unexpected generosity. But no serious threat to the dynasty could be tolerated.

For all his achievements – respect abroad, achieved through diplomacy rather than war, the quelling of disorder at home, the feat of survival itself – the continued existence of the dynasty hung by a thread and on one young man's life. The Tudors, for all their strength in governance, lacked the fecundity of their Plantagenet predecessors.

A man of high intelligence, Henry devoted himself to statecraft; of the business of governance he was the master. His objectives were rooted in a realistic appraisal of a given situation. In all this, and in his employment of conspicuously able men – some from quite humble backgrounds – there is a good deal in common with his great predecessor Henry I (as indeed in the loss of his son and heir), a man likewise berated for 'avarice' (evidently an occupational hazard). No great innovator himself, Henry VII took the existing machinery and used it effectively.

Francis Bacon, ever insightful, spoke of Henry VII as 'a wonder for wise men'; a politician's politician, 'what he minded he compassed'. If Henry died 'respected but unloved', would he have minded? Probably he would have taken it as a compliment.

CHAPTER 9

HENRY VIII (1509-1547)

Henry VIII

Henry is the 'lady killer' (quite literally so) of English monarchs. One man's love for a woman, whom he later had killed, helped to overthrow the barely questioned norms of centuries. Thomas More's metaphor on this man Henry is apposite: 'If a lion knew his own strength, hard were it for any man to rule him.' Henry was certainly masterful, at the same time volatile and suggestible; a supreme egotist driven by an all-consuming self-righteousness: traits not unknown in politicians of any era.

Human tragedy seems to lie close to the heart of the reign. One may picture a prematurely old man, his mind still clear, capricious and masterful, his bullock body racked with pain (from mishaps in the tiltyard especially). His mind turns to Anne Boleyn, once the great passion of his life, to his children Mary and Elizabeth, and to Edward, the hope of his dynasty. A tragedy above all for the myriad of human beings, great and small, informed and bewildered, their lives disrupted or destroyed, who were caught in the eye of the storm. But that is to anticipate. At the start all was hope.

The reign began in a blaze of expectation. The old king's 'heavy lordship' was at an end. 'Avarice' was banished from the realm. The country had entered 'a golden world', so said Cardinal Wolsey's biographer George Cavendish. A Venetian thought Henry the 'handsomest potentate I ever set eyes upon'. Still, there were straws in the wind: the judicial murders of Empson and Dudley, his father's loyal if over-zealous 'enforcers' – greeted, of course, with a chorus of adulation; and (rather later) of the duke of Buckingham, whose lineage and pretensions might conceivably pose a threat to the Tudor dynasty. Henry was almost paranoid about such things. The quest for a healthy male heir is a leitmotif running through the greater part of the reign.

Two other young monarchs, Henry's contemporaries Francis I of France and the Emperor Charles V (slightly younger and easily underrated) were no less anxious than the English king to strut their stuff, vying with each other, on the European stage; their counterpoint, over more than three decades, lends a certain unity to the times. That Charles was also Queen Catherine of Aragon's nephew, and king of Spain, was to be of crucial significance.

Henry's attention to business, notably in his early years, was fitful; such tedious matters came a poor second to the more seductive pleasures of the chase; the tiltyard, tennis, archery, theology, astronomy and music – the king was a gifted musician who particularly excelled at the lute – were other enduring passions. How fortunate he was to have the great cardinal, Thomas Wolsey, his 'loving friend', to rely on! – or so it seemed. Wolsey: omnicompetent, expansive, a lover of projects (especially buildings), optimistic, indefatigable; but also over-confident and over-stretched. [Fast forward 500 years. 4.00 a.m.: the barrage of emails – the bane of modern life – starts up from The Office of the Cardinal. And – God help us! – the millions of 'followers'!]

Yet the king was always capable of decisive intervention; and his judgement, by and large, was shrewd enough. Henry, perhaps surprisingly, seems to have retained an affection for his 'friend' the cardinal, even as the vultures gathered near the end. Wolsey in short was the man, to use that debased contemporary parlance, to 'get the job done'. Until, that is, the king's Great Matter, the divorce from Queen Catherine, ruined him: Wolsey's failure to procure a papal declaration invalidating the marriage sealed his fate.

On the continent, in Germany especially, the pope's authority was increasingly being challenged. From the second decade of the sixteenth century new ways of understanding faith through the scriptures, commonly associated with the name of Martin Luther, were steadily, even remarkably, gaining ground. Some German princes, keen to assert themselves vis-à-vis the emperor (who remained staunchly catholic), were especially receptive. The movement that came to be known as the protestant Reformation was beginning to take shape.

It is a supreme irony that Henry, a voracious reader of theology, had been held in special favour by a grateful pope. The title 'Defender of the Faith' was testimony to the king's unflagging zeal in defending papal claims against the rising Lutheran heresy in Germany.

The king's Great Matter became a cause célèbre across Europe. Henry had had 'scruples' of conscience about his marriage for quite a while. What had become of his anticipated male heir? Was his marriage, though sanctioned by the pope, not valid in God's eyes? Readings of Biblical texts reinforced his scruples. His late brother Arthur had, after all, also been married to Catherine. Had Arthur and Catherine 'carnally known' each other? Catherine absolutely denied it, but no one knew for sure. One thing was clear enough: the possibility of a healthy son by Catherine was now remote. This realisation drove Henry's obsessive campaign for an annulment of his marriage. And by now, around 1525, Henry was 'stricken with the dart of love' for another woman, Anne Boleyn. Henry had had mistresses before (including Anne's own sister) but such liaisons could not produce legitimate heirs. Anne, dark-eyed, vivacious, self-confident, outspoken was utterly different. And – she would only consent to be Henry's wife, not his mistress. She was so unlike Catherine (probably by now dowdy and rather boring)!

In May 1527 the Emperor Charles V's forces sacked Rome and the pope became Charles' prisoner. Charles, as Catherine's nephew, now found himself in a position to block any favourable response from the pope to Henry's pleas. Self-evidently the whole divorce strategy now had to be entirely re-appraised.

Thomas Cromwell was King Henry's other great minister. That he and the cardinal were close is evidenced in Wolsey's Gentleman-Usher George Cavendish's 'Life' of his master. Cromwell did much to salvage what he could of his friend's affairs following his fall; this will have brought him to the notice of the king. Cromwell, essentially Wolsey's man of affairs, gave sound and practical advice. Alas, the cardinal, ever the optimist, had never accepted the finality of his dismissal, even after his indictment as papal legate for 'praemunire' (the offence of illegally bringing papal jurisdiction into England). Henry, still showing tokens of favour, had allowed him to retire to his archdiocese of York (where, it is said, he had never set foot). Cromwell urged him to keep a low profile, to serve God, and stay out of politics. But intrigue was second nature to Wolsey. Still angling for a triumphal return to centre stage, he engaged in rash and treasonous communications. Arrested in York for treason, he died (November 1530) at Leicester on his journey south to the Tower. Anne Boleyn ('the night crow' Wolsey called her) will surely have rejoiced!

Thomas More, a lawyer by training, a layman, hugely respected (in particular by Queen Catherine) and intimate with the king, replaced Wolsey as lord chancellor. With his hallmark prescience, More was probably most reluctant to accept this honour. He knew well enough that the back-slapping camaraderie, the arm-in-arm perambulations of his Chelsea garden were but one side of this king; his master would have his head if it could 'win him a castle in France'. True to form, Henry subsequently perjured himself by reneging on his promise not to 'molest' More's conscience over the divorce. Thomas More was a devout catholic, a loyal son of the Church (and the pope). His heart was in his family, in Chelsea; and, too, in rebutting the arguments of the Lutheran heretics. And More was an unequivocal supporter of Catherine's cause.

Thomas Cranmer and Edward Foxe, Cambridge academics both, set before Henry a dossier making startling claims: the pope was simply 'bishop of Rome', no more; the king was supreme in England, clergy and laity being subject to him; and Henry was no less than Christ's deputy on earth. Music, surely, to Henry's ears! Then, in January 1533, Cranmer was appointed to the see of Canterbury.

What are we to make of Henry's own beliefs? 'Catholicism without the pope' seems close enough to the mark. In many respects he was deeply conservative: he believed in the Real Presence in the Sacrament and approved of clerical celibacy – ironically, Archbishop Cranmer was himself a married man! At the same time there was the capacity to move crab-like in different directions. As a result no one about court really knew where they stood – a situation Henry probably relished and a game at which he was remarkably adept. No one could ever feel truly safe.

Thomas Cranmer, by contrast, was strongly committed to the cause of religious reform; a position he shared with both Anne Boleyn and his friend Thomas Cromwell. Cranmer's uncompromising and unwavering belief in the royal supremacy was what, above all, commended him to his monarch and a warm personal relationship developed. (Their personal connection bears comparison with that of Henry IV and Archbishop Thomas Arundel more than 100 years before.) At crucial moments Henry intervened decisively to confound religious conservatives bent on his archbishop's overthrow. Politics was not Cranmer's home turf – he left such things to Cromwell. He would obligingly annul no fewer than three of the king's marriages. Henry always retained an almost touching faith in marriage, provided that no 'just impediment' was involved. In the political sphere, and as his career progressed, subservience to royal authority would prove Cranmer's defining characteristic. Still, charges of 'toadyism' can be pushed too far: the archbishop wrote brave letters in defence of both Anne Boleyn and Cromwell when they lay under condemnation in the Tower. Whether or not Henry actually saw these letters is unclear; what is certain is that they made no difference.

*   *   *

Politically the events of 1532 – severing the historic ties with Rome – were decisive: the constitutional independence of the Church was destroyed; and the clergy accepted the king (not the pope) as their supreme legislator. It was then, too, that Thomas More resigned as chancellor and retired into private life. In January 1533 Henry secretly married Anne. That March the Act in Restraint of Appeals to Rome made it possible to settle the divorce in England; its preamble asserted 'that this realm of England is an empire ... governed by one Supreme Head and King'. Cranmer declared the marriage with Catherine to be void and that with Anne true; on 1 June Anne was crowned queen. Catherine and Henry's daughter Mary (born 1516) was therefore illegitimate and the crown must descend to the children of Henry and Anne. An oath was imposed throughout the kingdom acknowledging Henry's new marriage and its offspring. It was now declared treasonable to call the king or queen heretic or schismatic. The Act of Supremacy unconditionally declared Henry head on earth of the Church of England. This legislation marked the triumph of the secular state over the Church.

Thomas Cromwell's agency can readily be discerned in drafting and piloting this revolutionary programme, enacted at breakneck speed, through parliament. The political sovereignty created by these Reformation statutes was a parliamentary one. Henry, massive egotist though he was, could not play the role of despot. One can readily believe that this partnership between king and parliament was a source of real pride to Henry; certainly he made sure that its members were fully implicated in this programme.

Within weeks of making himself supreme head of the Church, Henry appointed Cromwell his vicar-general (his deputy) in spiritual affairs. What massive confidence he placed in this man, son of a Putney tavern-keeper/brewer! And Cromwell worked prodigiously fast overhauling the machinery of government.

Yet Cromwell, for all his pre-eminence, was for two reasons more vulnerable than Wolsey had ever been: unlike the cardinal, he was never Henry's 'friend'; and, like Cranmer, he wanted to push the reform agenda forward more radically than his royal master would countenance, leading him into indiscreet, unauthorised contacts abroad. For about one thing Henry was always adamant: the direction of foreign policy was the province of the prince alone. Their relationship was turbulent; the hot-tempered king was not past giving Cromwell a good 'pummelling' when it suited him.

Meanwhile, Cromwell's understanding with Anne had begun to unravel. In a remarkably daring move – for reasons essentially connected with his own survival – the minister changed sides and allied himself with his former conservative adversaries, and those whose sympathies were not at all with the queen. His high-risk strategy paid off brilliantly. In May 1536 Anne was executed on trumped-up charges of adultery and incest; her brother George and also her friends – all of them probably innocent – were likewise caught in Cromwell's web. The men taken, genuinely bewildered at the fate that had overtaken them, included some of Henry's closest intimates. One can believe that unguarded words and innuendos – understandable enough in the flirtatious and febrile world of 'courtly love' – were reported to Cromwell by the minister's network of informers. Henry, always suggestible and prone to paranoia, was now consumed by feelings of loathing towards Anne and lacerating self-pity. He needed little persuading of his wife's guilt. A compliant jury did the rest. And just before she died Cranmer's court at Lambeth reached the astonishing conclusion that Henry's adultery with Anne's sister had made the marriage invalid from the start!

In her lifetime Anne Boleyn was a deeply controversial figure. The butt of much ill-concealed public hostility, she never enjoyed the affection and sympathy accorded to Catherine of Aragon (who had herself died only four months previously). Still, if she had borne Henry that elusive son – it was left to Jane Seymour, Henry's next wife, to deliver on that – she would presumably have survived and indeed prospered. The miscarriage of a male child, following a jousting injury to her husband, was a personal disaster for the queen. Anne's place in history, though, is secure. But for Henry's passion and Anne's steely resolve that she would only consent to be the king's wife, not merely his mistress, the break from Rome would surely have followed a rather different course.

There is a heart-rending scene at Greenwich Palace recounted much later to Elizabeth by the cleric Alexander Alesius, an eye-witness: a public altercation between Henry and Anne, the baby princess Elizabeth in her arms, the queen in vain 'entreating the most serene king'; and the noise of the cannon heralding the arrival of a traitor in the Tower.

By and large the political and clerical classes accepted the revolutionary constitutional changes. The alternative – a martyr's crown – was for most not an attractive option. There were, of course, those who might now be termed 'refuseniks': pre-eminent were Thomas More, Henry's sometime friend, and John Fisher, the revered and ascetic bishop of Rochester, a fearless defender of Catherine's cause; such men as these were prepared (if reluctantly) to swear to the oath to the succession as laid down in parliament, but not to the condemnation of the first marriage and (by implication) a denial of papal supremacy. Fisher was beheaded in June 1535, More ('I die the king's faithful servant, but God's first') the month after. For the same reason the Carthusian monks, renowned for the holiness of their lives, suffered the death of traitors; they were dragged, following unspeakable ill-treatment, on hurdles from the Tower to Tyburn. European opinion was horrified. With good reason these killings are regarded as among the worst blots on Henry's record.

Cromwell, by means of a really professional bureaucratic machine, set to the task of taking a census of the wealth of the monasteries (not to mention, through his agents, a list of their alleged laxity and corruption). The Church owned perhaps between a quarter and a third of all land in England. The dissolution of the monasteries offered rich pickings for ambitious men on the make, who were not slow to avail themselves of the high quality building materials on offer; and windfalls, too, for the crown's far from healthy finances. In the end all that remained were the 'bare ruined choirs'. This gigantic redistribution of land has no parallel in English history, at least since the Norman Conquest. Cromwell desired, above all, to ensure that the crown would be permanently and securely endowed.

A sudden storm of opposition – known as the Pilgrimage of Grace – convulsed Lincolnshire, Yorkshire, and the north more generally in late 1536. The protesters, some 40,000 in number, were in arms about religious changes and the dissolutions; agrarian unrest, enclosures and raised rents were probably also issues. The rising rocked the Henrician order to its foundations. The religious feelings of the people were mostly (especially outside London) conservative and catholic. Many were shocked at the image-breaking of Cromwell's commissioners. The rising might even have succeeded if its 'chief captain', the lawyer Robert Aske, had not been so naively trusting of the king's goodwill.

In the end the Pilgrimage was crushed with exemplary brutality: Henry ordered the reprisals to be 'without pity or respect'. At Canterbury the shrine of Thomas Becket, England's premier saint, a martyr for the Church's liberty against encroaching royal power, was dismantled, quantities of treasure removed and the saint's bones burnt. Becket represented everything Henry most loathed. A new play 'On the Treason of Becket' by an ex-friar was performed to mark the king's visit to the city.

One crucial question remained, however: Who could provide salvation following the removal of papal authority? Cranmer's answer was that the people must save their own souls by having faith in the merits of Christ. And, in a reversal of his previous policy that had led to the death of the translator William Tyndale, Henry gave the English Bible – a copy to be displayed in every church – to the people.

After Anne Boleyn, Henry's next three marriages were (for different reasons) short-lived affairs. The débâcle of the second, to Anne of Cleves, was largely responsible for the demise of Thomas Cromwell. This Anne – for political and religious reasons – was the minister's preferred match, but the choice finally was the king's. That Henry took such an instant dislike to Anne and could not be 'carnally aroused' was scarcely Cromwell's fault! The likelihood is that Henry was, or became, partially impotent. The testimony of George Boleyn at his own trial made oblique reference to this – and caused a sensation. It is known that doubts about the king's vigour – however dangerous to express them – were circulating.

Between 1509 and 1547 Henry is known (or may be presumed) to have had sexual relations with eight women: his six wives and his two known mistresses, Elizabeth Blount and Mary Boleyn. Only four pregnancies produced a healthy infant. Henry did not suffer from syphilis.

Henry's fifth marriage, to Catherine Howard, a young niece – like Anne Boleyn – of the duke of Norfolk, a leading magnate, conservative in religion and probably Cromwell's most implacable enemy at court, shows the king as the volatile and suggestible being he was. In this, and much else besides, how different from his father! Marriage to a young and vivacious woman might, on the rebound from the Cleves disaster, bring much sought after rejuvenation. Vain hope! Disillusion, when it came – the charge, inevitably, one of adultery – was bitter indeed! Henry's disposal of Catherine, at the hands of the executioner, reveals as much as anything the strong vein of cruelty that ran through his character. The septuagenarian duke of Norfolk, a dutiful long-term servant of his royal master, was himself only saved from execution by Henry's timely death (28 January 1547).

Allowing himself to be 'bounced' into having his greatest minister killed on trumped-up charges – the execution itself was horribly botched – was arguably Henry's greatest mistake, and one that he belatedly seems to have come to realise. Men of noble lineage – the king's 'natural' counsellors – bridled at being under the subjection of men of 'base' origins, 'foul churls' like Cromwell or, before him, Wolsey. And Cromwell too seems to have had a constructive vision of an efficiently ordered Christian polity (or 'common weal'), quite beyond the grasp of his adversaries; his extensive and wide-ranging legislative plans bear this out. With the great minister gone, the reign seems to have lost a sense of purpose. Certainly Cromwell had no successor. Henry resumed his favourite pastime: war, now with the Scots and the French. It was finally futile, prodigal both of lives and resources – though the demand for armaments gave a fillip to the iron industry in the Sussex Weald.

Henry's final marriage, to Catherine Parr, possibly more of a companionable affair, was actually quite sensible, at least from his point of view. As for Catherine, marriage to a gross, physically intimidating hulk of a man, and with a track record of cruelty, was not a vocation to be entered into lightly. No doubt, though, the easy charm, the bluff affability could readily be turned on still. Catherine was probably safe enough, as long as she stayed clear of theology (her husband's particular province).

For close on 40 years Henry had kept his subjects in his thrall. To the end he was masterful, capricious and dangerous: a combination that none of his predecessors of the same name had manifested. Probably he always retained much of his popularity. For the king, ever cocksure, well understood and his mindset chimed in with the temper of his people: essentially conservative and with a burgeoning national pride. Henry's impressive development of the English navy is fully in keeping with this swagger. Anyway, if things went awry, scapegoats ('evil counsellors' and the like) were not hard to find. But now the prospect of a royal minority must have been viewed with acute concern and foreboding. That Henry chose evangelical tutors for his son Edward suggests (though with Henry one can never be sure) that his mind was moving in the direction of reform, if not remotely at the pace his ever-faithful friend Archbishop Thomas Cranmer so earnestly desired.

And it was Cranmer – always at his best in a pastoral role – who was there at the end to see him on his final journey to whatever may lie beyond.

EPILOGUE

As for a Henry IX? It is a fact that, but for his tragically early death (1612), the burden of kingship would have fallen upon Henry prince of Wales (rather than his brother Charles), son of King James I. The parallel is irresistible: if Prince Arthur had lived, would there have been a Reformation in England; and, if Prince Henry, an English Civil War? But such speculation is not the business of any reputable writer of history, a craft which Dr Johnson for one held in relatively low regard.

Finally, in the eighteenth century there was Henry Stuart Cardinal Duke of York, grandson of King James II, the final Stuart pretender to publicly claim the throne. Known to his devotees as Henry IX, he prudently made no effort, however, to make good his claim.

Still the show, even in the absence of Henrys, carries on: the Monarchy, its buttress the ever-faithful Church of England. 'Present, past and future in one mighty roll!' Words taken from a 'school song', symbolic of the risible pretensions of a Black Country grammar school of unblessed memory, feel apposite. 'Always play the game!' Amen, I say to that. Amen indeed!

One general conclusion is inescapable: where barons and political elites were concerned, the twelfth century was more civilised – and safer – than those that followed. By any standards the first two Henrys, when all necessary reservations are made, were responsible monarchs of very high calibre. The real decline set in with the reign of Edward I who started up politically motivated killings of men of high standing, including the subjugated Welsh and the Scots. Under his inadequate successor things got infinitely worse. The situation reached its nadir in the blood-letting of the Wars of the Roses, either on the battlefield or in the murderous settling of scores that followed – the conflict largely brought about by the presence of a manifestly incapable king. For Henry VII, that somewhat wry monarch of high intelligence, the ultimate penalty was only discriminatingly employed, as a last resort; for his rather frightening son it came close to becoming the first. All this while the overwhelming majority of people, those outside the political elite, got on with their lives as best as they could; but then this has always been so.

Mindful of the tragic and transitory nature of human life, it has seemed to me fitting to close with a prayer attributed to King Henry VI, a man most sorely afflicted upon 'the rack of this tough world', but whose architectural legacy continues to inspire wonder and amazement:

'O Lord Jesus Christ, who hast created and redeemed me and hast foreordained me unto that which now I am; thou knowest what thou wouldst do with me; do with me according to thy will, in thy mercy. Amen.'